RELATIONSHIP

RELATIONSHIP

The Essence of Discipleship

JAKE GIESBRECHT

Printed in Canada

ISBN: 978-1-4866-1789-0

Word Alive Press
119 De Baets Street, Winnipeg, MB R2J 3R9
www.wordalivepress.ca

Cataloguing in Publication may be obtained through Library and Archives Canada

CONTENTS

ACKNOWLEDGEMENTS

I must mention first my wife, Ruth, who has been a great source of encouragement over the years of ministry, and in the work of research and writing of this book. She took on the task of editing and trying to shape my sentences and paragraphs into proper form while trying to keep in mind my thinking process. She has been willing to challenge me where needed and has given very helpful feedback. That has been done thoroughly, and sometimes humourously.

I have appreciated the editing work of my sister, Freda Bostrom, who has varied experiences in the art of composition. Many thanks for your effort and diligence.

I was very thankful for the insightful and detailed work of editing by Paul Sheppard, a retired English teacher. His many suggestions and corrections made for a book that is easier to read. He was not afraid to take extra time to clarify many of his suggestions.

I value the input from a good friend, Dennis Thomson, who gave me good feedback on the content, and made suggestions, both in content and style, that are based on a very strong friendship.

INTRODUCTION

While many people who attend church today give verbal assent to the gospel, they are not equipped to serve. Ephesians 4:11–12 and 2 Timothy 3:16–17 speak distinctly to the issue of the equipping of believers for good works and service.

Other believers are taken up with distractions that occupy their time and energy. In our modern age, distractions have become a major factor in our society. There is need for Christians to commit to pursuing a walk with Christ above all else.

We need to recognize that the element of intentional discipleship is often missing in the Church. This discipline must be embraced in order to bring believers to a place where they can serve in the strength of their gifting.

Our first priority is the need for a biblical understanding of the nature of discipleship, and how it has been exercised. In the process of this practice of discipleship, others will learn and be equipped to pursue the same objective, namely, that of discipling believers to spiritual growth and commitment to serving others in the name of the Lord.

Various passages of Scripture will be examined to show that this approach follows the authority of the Word of God.

We live in a church culture where personal opinions are valued too highly. Unfortunately, these opinions have taken away from understanding of the Word of God, and our commitment to its authenticity and authority.

I first saw discipleship in practice in the beginning of my pastoral ministry. My senior pastor demonstrated discipleship among some of the men in the church. I have seen the value of discipleship as I've watched men and women who were discipled stay active in the spiritual development of other men and women. I have practiced discipleship as I have been able, although I was too busy in ordinary church life to practice it as I now understand its importance. If I had to do it all over again, I would place discipleship much higher on my list of priorities.

I have seen the results of discipleship in the lives of people. I find the greatest joy in this ministry. It is a delight to see the effects discipleship has on individuals, particularly as it leads men and women to give themselves to ministry and leadership, whether formal or informal.

It may be profitable to remember that men ought to disciple men and women ought to disciple women. This practice speaks to a high standard of integrity in the matter of male/female relationships.

I want to do whatever I can to make the Church aware of the need of intentional discipleship. It is my hope that this book will demonstrate my passion for that ministry.

I also want to offer a word of caution: in North America, we have lived in a freedom from challenges to our faith which has often made us insensitive to changes that are happening in our culture, in both church and secular society. This has made us vulnerable to being conformed to the world by not holding us accountable to the biblical standard of truth and conduct. Government, society and church are making changes at an alarming speed. I see discipleship as a major defense against conformity to the world.

That followers of Christ in Western culture will be persecuted is hardly in doubt. When that happens, governments may try to shut down the Church, but they will only be able to shut down buildings. Jesus said, "*I will build my church*" (Matthew 16:18) and no humans or human organizations will be able to shut it down.

It is tragic when we identify church as a building but when buildings are shut down, followers of Christ will realize to a greater degree our dependence on each other. By necessity, we will meet together in smaller venues, primarily in homes where we will intentionally nurture each other in the various aspects of following Jesus Christ. This may well cause the Church to become more committed to following its mandate.

This book is meant to be informational and motivational. It will not set out a pattern to follow. It will not seek to set out a program of discipleship. As you will see, I believe we must resist the concept of program, and instead focus on relationship.

Discipleship is relational. Every discipleship experience will be unique as it seeks to meet the needs of individuals. How this might be done we will see in various discussions throughout the book.

This book is meant to begin a conversation. It is meant to cause thorough study and deep reflective thought that leads to action.

Chapter One

DISCIPLESHIP BASIS

MY WIFE AND I DRIVE ALONG A COUNTRY ROAD ON THE WAY TO THE church we attend. One spring we noticed heavy equipment on a tract of land of a couple of hundred hectares that was seemingly quite useless. It was scruffy, containing a mixture of trees and rocks, and having no apparent productive value at all. The equipment was removing rocks, cutting down trees, pulling up trunks and root systems, and piling them up to be burned.

The next thing we noticed was the presence of tiling equipment and miles of drain tile, which is buried underground to provide drainage in the case of heavy rains. After the tiling was completed, the land was leveled off, seemingly ready for the planting of crops.

Sure enough, in a week or two we saw signs of seeding having taken place, and in another week or two we saw growth. At the time of writing, the field had a great crop of corn growing and maturing. It has been a delight to see the transformation from a totally unproductive piece of land into something productive and pleasant to observe.

This process reminded me very much of what happens in the process of discipleship.

But what do I mean when I say discipleship? Let's begin with a personal definition so that you don't need guesswork while reading this book. The definition I use in this book comes out of observation of Scriptural practices and personal experiences in terms of being discipled:

Discipleship occurs when a believer in Jesus Christ intentionally commits himself or herself to walking with another believer to assist in the development of that believer's character, to see that believer's character fashioned into the character of Christ by a growing knowledge of and obedience to Scripture.

In *The Great Omission,* author and philosopher Dallas Willard claims that discipleship has been omitted from our North American church practice and jargon. If he is right, what are we actually missing? The answer is found in Scripture, where discipleship is a key principle and Matthew 28:18-20 is a key text:

And Jesus came and spoke to them, saying, "All authority has been given to Me in heaven and on earth. Go therefore and make disciples of all the nations, baptizing them in the name of the Father and of the Son and of the Holy Spirit, teaching them to observe all things that I have commanded you; and lo, I am with you always, even to the end of the age."

This passage is critical for we are dealing here with Jesus's last words to the Church. These final words—known as the Great Commission—are not merely suggestions for the Church to consider but are our marching orders. Jesus expects to be obeyed by those who would follow Him. It is not optional.

The language around "making disciples" is powerfully focused on the disciple, or pupil. As we trace the teachings of Jesus and the Apostle Paul through the New Testament, we will stress the intent in Jesus's words. We can see this intention not only in what they taught, but also what they practised.

It is important to note that the call from Jesus in this text is not one to evangelism, although that is part of the exercise of being a follower of Jesus Christ. Jesus said in Matthew 4:19, "*Follow me, and I will make you fishers of men.*" When discipleship is viewed and practiced biblically, evangelism will follow in the life of the disciple. There must be an intertwining between evangelism and discipleship. If a disciple's life is given to both the growth of individuals in the Christian faith, and in the Church of Jesus Christ, evangelism will be an essential ingredient in that life.

Two terms will be used interchangeably to make the point that discipleship is Jesus's way for church growth. The two terms are discipleship and nurturing. These are meaningful aspects of the lifestyle of following Christ. The term lifestyle is used advisedly: discipleship is not a *program*, but a *lifestyle*. It is not something that is pre-programmed, nor an occasional exercise. It must become a commitment to a way of life.

As a side note, let me say that I had considered using the word mentoring as well, but careful consideration led me to not include it. A mentor, by dictionary definition is a "trusted and experienced adviser,"[1] but I will contend that discipleship has a component that is not necessarily included in mentoring. That component is the spiritual element of life change.

A job description was issued by a church in Ontario, Canada for a discipleship coordinator position. It read:

> The Discipleship Coordinator will develop, organize, supervise and execute programs and events relating to educating and equipping children, youth, adults and families to promote and enrich Christian life, work, and witness.

I believe that job description is missing even a remote resemblance to discipleship. Instead it describes programs. I also believe that discipleship is not a program to be followed, but a relationship with individuals.

Author Robert Coleman says the following:

> Jesus came to save the world, and to that end He died, but on his way to the Cross He concentrated His life on making a few disciples. These men were taught to do the same, until through the process of

---

1 Reader's Digest Oxford Complete Wordfinder, The Reader's Digest Association Inc., Pleasantville, NY, 1993, p. 936

reproduction, the gospel of the kingdom would reach to the ends of the earth.[2]

This fits well with what Jesus commands the Church to do in Matthew 28:18–20: to go and make disciples.

People tend to view the text in Matthew as Jesus *inviting* believers to go and make disciples. We accept an invitation only after having evaluated and then made a decision to accept it. But I contend that this is a command, not an invitation, and that our only response ought to be obedience. We will further explore this in an attempt to gain an understanding of what it is to follow the Master. The reality is that Jesus does not invite us to go; He commands us to go. This connects with a fundamental understanding of the Lordship of Jesus Christ. A believer does not decide to make Jesus Lord; He is and always will be Lord. The only question is our response. In Luke 6:46, Jesus says, "*But why do you call me 'Lord, Lord,' and not do the things which I say?*" Philippians 2:9–11 also makes the point that Jesus will always be Lord:

> *Therefore God also has highly exalted Him and given Him the name which is above every name, that at the name of Jesus every knee should bow, of those in heaven, and of those on earth, and of those under the earth, and that every tongue*

---

2 Leroy Eims, *The Lost Art of Disciple Making,* Zondervan, Grand Rapids, Mich. 1978, p.9

should confess that Jesus Christ is Lord, to the glory of God the Father.

When I came to faith in Christ and His redemptive work on the Cross, God opened my eyes to His Lordship and I surrendered to Him as Lord. This was not (and is not) a multiple-choice arrangement. The same pattern is seen in the lives of the Apostle Paul (Acts 9), the Philippian jailer (Acts 16), and the Ethiopian eunuch (Acts 8), to mention a few. Disciple-making has always been a matter of submission to the Lordship of Christ. Surrender is one step, followed by a life of ongoing transformation:

> *...do not be conformed to this world, but be transformed by the renewing of your mind, that you may prove what is that good and acceptable and perfect will of God.*
>
> —Romans 12:2

The fact of Jesus's ongoing Lordship is a fundamental truth we must recognize and act upon.

In the context of the Lordship of Jesus, David Platt says, "We create a nice non-offensive politically correct, middle class American Jesus, who looks like us and thinks like us."[3] What the Church practises does not speak well of His sovereign, eternal Lordship.

---

3   David Platt, *Follow Me,* Multnomah, Colorado Springs, Colorado, 2010, p.78

His Lordship is far above and beyond our comprehension, and places demands upon us that require obedience in response.

In Matthew 4:19 Jesus said to the called ones, *"Follow Me, and I will make you fishers of men."* He used imagery that they, as fishermen, would understand. Just as a fisherman knows that fish do not come seeking to be caught, so the follower of Christ needs to live a lifestyle in which he or she seeks out those who will benefit from discipleship.

Intentional discipleship is a mindset and a lifestyle. It is not an occasional effort at obeying Jesus's command to make disciples. We need to believe that this is Jesus's expectation for those who seek to be His followers.

I was discipled early on in my ministry, and as a result discipleship became a passion. When I was an assistant pastor, I served under a senior pastor who had a strong conviction about training men, and who discipled a number of younger men over the years. The benefit of that discipling caught my attention and has had an ongoing effect on my thinking and practice. I believe in discipleship theologically and have seen and experienced its benefits. Therefore, it is essential to see discipleship as an ongoing lifestyle for Christians, permeating all aspects of our everyday life.

Discipleship leads to evangelism because it leads to changed lives. As our transformation into the image of Christ takes place, we will sense a burden for the salvation of others. In fact, discipleship is related to every part of biblical living; it will influence how we see the lost state of those around us.

This call to a mindset of discipleship requires a change in North American church culture. Some components that are deeply entrenched in church culture need to be changed, will be difficult to evaluate and will be easy to dismiss if they are found wanting.

One of these components is a confusion between the terms "works" and "works righteousness." This is an important distinction and will be addressed in various chapters in this book. Some denominations have historically taken a very strong stand against "works righteousness," but in more recent times in North America the distinction has become blurred. "Works" refers to that which is done as a result of transformation, while "works righteousness" refers to works which are done in an attempt to gain redemption.

Discipleship places an emphasis on works done as a result of transformation. Jesus said to "*observe all things that I have commanded you*" (Matthew 28:20). Much of what Jesus commanded are actions or works. The verb "observe" in the Matthew command has a greater meaning than to simply notice something; it has to do with following through in action, as seen in the phrase "*observe to do*" which is found in Joshua 1:8. In Philippians 2:12, Paul says "*work out your own salvation*" which does not mean to work for your salvation. That assumption would be a serious contradiction to Ephesians 2:8–9 which says, "*For by grace you have been saved through faith, and that not of yourselves; it is the gift of God, not of works, lest anyone should boast*" and Titus 3:5 which talks of God's love which is "*not by works of righteousness which we have done, but according to His mercy He saved us, through the washing of regeneration and renewing of the Holy Spirit.*"

There may seem to be some contradiction between grace and effort, but when rightly understood there should not be a contradiction. Grace requires—or perhaps demands—effort, but not for earning standing or merit before God. Rather it requires effort in the working out of our faith. The Matthew 28:20 text demands effort, and discipleship demands doing, but that must begin with being. We will look at this in detail later.

Biblical exposition and personal experience have power to inform us, but if we want to transform character, this is where discipleship comes into play. Multitudes of people attending evangelical churches across North America appear to experience only minimal change in their lifestyle choices. This lack of transformation in large degree is due to the lack of accountability in their lives. They may know what needs to be done to walk in obedience to Christ, but lack direct accountability, and thus their awareness and perhaps desire for change quickly dissipates. My own testimony may be of help here. One of my great regrets about my younger years as a follower of Jesus Christ is the lack of intentional discipleship in my life, even though I was surrounded by good people who were relatively new believers. People were nurturing and related well to one another, but I know that I would have benefitted from someone coming alongside me to disciple me personally and intentionally.

Other words used for disciple include: learner, follower, student, and apprentice. All these terms relate to someone taking in information and being encouraged to develop character. Jesus was the master discipler. He showed us the urgency and the means of making disciples. We learn a lot about discipleship by reviewing instances where disciples learned from and followed Christ.

What Jesus expects in discipleship is not complicated or obscure. We don't need to complicate it with expectations or rules. Instead, reading and studying His life on earth will give us an understanding of the nature of discipleship. The New Testament is about disciples, by disciples, and for disciples. Just as in other areas of Christian living, we can have greater clarity about discipleship by committing as a church to reading and studying the Scriptures to see how Jesus worked while on earth.

One of the greatest issues in the North American church today is allowing discipleship to be optional. Being optional might be true if the call to following Jesus Christ was indeed only an invitation, but it is a command from the One to whom we owe total loyalty. Rather than simply attaining knowledge of the practice of discipleship, we are to engage in practices of discipleship. We can see these practices in the disciplines Jesus demonstrated in His own life. Consider briefly the following list:

Solitude: Jesus took time alone with God for reflection and meditation. This practice will break the power of busyness. We see examples of this in the following Scriptures: "*So He Himself often withdrew into the wilderness and prayed*"(Luke 5:16), and, "*Now it came to pass in those days that He went out to the mountain to pray, and continued all night in prayer to God*" (Luke 6:12).

Silence: God tells us to allow time when God speaks and we listen; "*Be still, and know that I am God*" (Psalm 46:10a). The purpose of that stillness is not to draw away from something, but to draw near to God.

Study: We need times of uninterrupted and concentrated study of a selected Scripture passage, or topic. There are three significant components of a study of Scripture: observation, interpretation, and application. It has been my experience that many Christians love Bible study, but want to hear the interpretation of a teacher, rather than taking the time to observe carefully what the text says. This is one key area in which people need to be discipled.

Service: As Jesus served in His divinity, healing and feeding people, we need to serve in ways that reflect His divinity.

Worship: Each of the above is done as an act of worship. This is the time when God Himself is the only object of our thoughts.

I can almost hear the objection, "If only I could find the time for these disciplines." The good news is that we don't need to *find* time. We all have exactly the same amount of time each day. What is needed is to *make* time. This is a matter of priority.

These practices are spiritual disciplines that are vital to a well-intentioned Christian life, although the list is not exhaustive. To quote Dallas Willard, "It is in these that the readiness to do evil that inhabits our body through long practice is gradually removed to an ever-increasing degree."[4] In the ministry of discipleship, nurturing each other is essential in practising these disciplines. Discipleship involves the disciple giving permission

---

4   Dallas Willard, *The Great Omission,* Monarch Books, Oxford U.K. 2006, p.21

to the discipler to evaluate honestly how he or she is growing in these practices. This nurturing becomes very significant in the development of godly character. These practices are also very valuable in the lives of those involved in discipleship ministry, and in the planting and encouraging of new churches (which is a welcome outcome of this focus on discipleship).

It is likely that this method of nurturing was what prepared the believers in Act 2 to become the instruments of church growth after they were scattered by persecution. We read in Acts 8:1: "…*at that time a great persecution arose against the church which was at Jerusalem; and they were all scattered throughout the regions of Judea and Samaria, except the apostles*." Persecution drove the believers to other regions where they planted churches. It is noteworthy that it was common believers who went out to do the task, not the apostles. It is evident from Acts 2:41–47 that the believers spent a lot of time together, during which time this ministry of *"teaching and admonishing one another"* (Colossians 3:16) took place. Perhaps it needs to be said that the church should be prepared to go into the world without waiting to be motivated by persecution, but in the case of Acts, persecution was the driving force. The whole church was trained by the process of nurturing each other, thus the believers were ready when the call came to go to other regions. 1 Corinthians 3:16 speaks to this reality as well: "*Do you not know that you are the temple of God and that the Spirit of God dwells in you?*"

The curriculum for discipleship must be the Bible. A discipling relationship will focus on many questions of life, with answers coming from convictions developed through a study of Scripture, and obedience to what it teaches rather than from public opinion, fanciful interpretation, or even material that can be picked off the shelves in a Christian bookstore. An understanding of discipleship begins with a study of 2 Timothy 3:16–17:

> *All Scripture is given by inspiration of God, and is profitable for doctrine, for reproof, for correction, for instruction in righteousness, that the man of God may be complete, thoroughly equipped for every good work.*

This verse offers us six elements that prepare us for the task of discipleship. The verse declares the Word of God is inspired, instructional, reproving, corrective, profitable, and equipping. Instruction is a key element in this list and comes in two areas: instruction in doctrine, and instruction in righteousness. Righteousness has to do with character and action, not merely knowledge.

When will the people of God receive this valued and necessary instruction? Will Sunday services suffice to provide the training and equipping needed? Note that the fellowship and nurturing in the church was evidently very extensive in Acts 2. This nurturing must be done in the form of accountability and application, which happens most profitably in discipleship.

A brief look at responses to God's Word point to the need for enhancing our knowledge of Scripture. The very first recorded encounter Satan had with humanity is described in Genesis 3:1 where his first question to Eve was, *"Has God really said?"*

Doubt was instilled in the human heart right from the beginning, and it has captured the imagination of the North American church today, with Bible reading among church attendees dropping. Another response to the Word of God can be seen in 2 Chronicles 36:16, where mockery of the Book was seen as the answer: "*But they mocked the messengers of God, despised His words, and scoffed at His prophets, until the wrath of the Lord arose against His people, till there was no remedy.*" In Jeremiah 36:1–25, the answer lay in burning the book of the Law. It would be helpful for the reader to study this passage from Jeremiah before proceeding further in the reading of this book.

The practice of discipleship and nurturing needs to be based on an honest, believing response to God's Word. Otherwise we are merely asking people to follow a personal, secular, self-promoting lifestyle with its own agenda, goals, and ambitions.

Chapter Two

DISCIPLESHIP IN HISTORY

SOME CHURCHES HAVE A CULTURE OF SPIRITUAL FORMATION, WHERE A ministry of nurture and discipleship is vibrant. This ministry is described in Ephesians 4:11–16:

> *And He Himself gave some to be apostles, some prophets, some evangelists, and some pastors and teachers, for the equipping of the saints for the work of ministry, for the edifying of the body of Christ, till we all come to the unity of the faith and of the knowledge of the Son of God, to a perfect man, to the measure of the stature of the fullness of Christ; that we should no longer be children, tossed to and fro and carried about with every wind of doctrine, by the trickery of men, in the cunning craftiness of deceitful plotting, but, speaking the truth in love, may grow up in all things into Him who is the head—Christ—from whom the whole body, joined and knit together by what every joint supplies, according to the effective working by which every part does its share, causes growth of the body for the edifying of itself in love.*

Three principles are clear in this passage, pointing out the purposes of the church and its members. First, the saints are being equipped to minister to each other. Second, the equipping enables the work of the ministry to be done. The third result is that the church will be edified, being spiritually enriched and ultimately growing in numbers, although numbers ought not to be the goal but rather the result of this work. The text indicates a growing Christlikeness of a church steadfast in doctrine, joined together for effectiveness.

There is a certain beauty and strength in the description of the church as "*knit together by what every joint supplies*" (Ephesians 4:16). Two elements in that statement stand out: the fact of being knit together, and the provision of resources from "every joint."

This knitting and supplying does not happen hastily, or in a short period of time. It is the process we will call spiritual formation which is the formation of spiritual character. Dallas Willard enlarges on this thought when he writes, "Spiritual formation is the process through which those who love and trust Jesus effectively take on His character."[5] Spiritual formation is the process which will bring about discipleship ministry.

---

5   Dallas Willard, *The Great Omission*, Monarch Books, Oxford U.K. 2014, p.80

Author James C. Wilhoit states that some of the practices of spiritual formation have become stale and unattractive. He laments the erosion of intentional practices of spiritual formation.[6]

Dallas Willard states that spiritual formation must not be grounded merely in spiritual abstractions but in the life, teaching, and ministry of Jesus. It must then find its source in the teaching of Jesus in the New Testament, and as recorded throughout Scripture. The practices of systematic Bible teaching, Bible memorization, hospitality, pastoral visitation, and intergenerational socializing are some of the elements that made up the practice of formation and discipleship in the past, but which have been discarded.

The "frog in the kettle" principle comes into play here. This principle states that if you toss a frog in boiling water it will try to jump out. But if a frog placed in cold water which is gradually warmed up to boiling, the frog will adapt and stay put. So the church has slowly experienced the erosion of these discipleship practices, not becoming alarmed about the change because it has been gradual, subtle, and thus effective. It has taken generations to effectively tear down and discard the principles of discipleship and will likely take generations to restore them again. The way to battle spiritual decline in the church is for all believers to invest time and energy in one other.[7] When this is

---

6 James C. Wilhoit, *Spiritual Formation as if the Church Mattered,* Baker Publishing, Grand Rapids, Mich, p.14

7 Ibid, p.34

not done, rot sets in. To avoid spiritual decay, we must nurture each other for the sake of the body.[8] This practice of nurturing will be the theme of a later chapter.

One key element needing to be stressed in discipleship studies is intentionality in church ministry. As part of this process we will revisit the history of discipleship. My own experience, which is probably similar to that of many on the journey of spiritual formation, is that of discrediting and discarding tradition. When tradition is taught in alignment with biblical truth, it solidifies our spiritual foundation. Jesus saw this foundation to be a vitally important component to the life of faith, saying,

> *Therefore whoever hears these sayings of Mine, and does them, I will liken him to a wise man who built his house on the rock: and the rain descended, the floods came, and the winds blew and beat on that house; and it did not fall, for it was founded on the rock. But everyone who hears these sayings of Mine, and does not do them, will be like a foolish man who built his house on the sand: and the rain descended, the floods came, and the winds blew and beat on that house; and it fell. And great was its fall."*
>
> —Matthew 7:24–27

The purpose of Jewish education was to establish this foundation so that people would never forget God or their history,

---

8   Ibid, p.34

and would therefore always be obedient to follow His commandments: *"When all that generation had been gathered to their fathers, another generation arose after them who did not know the Lord nor the work which He had done for Israel,"* (Judges 2:10); *"And you shall remember that you were a slave in Egypt, and you shall be careful to observe these statutes"* (Deuteronomy 16:12).

I find it profitable to view discipleship in the contexts of the rabbinical system of the Old Testament, and the ongoing Jewish system of today. The term rabbi was taken seriously by the rabbis in Jewish history and has traditionally been translated master or teacher. These are fitting titles for Jesus Christ.

The nature of what it means to be a teacher is also important. Anyone who wishes to have an influence on students must see himself or herself not as a teacher of information, but as a teacher of students. Discipleship is not taught; students are taught about discipleship. Teachers do not teach how to study the Bible; teachers teach students how to study the Bible. These are important distinctions that help give perspective to the focus on individuals or small groups when considering and practising discipleship. This distinction goes back to the rabbinical system where the focus of Jewish training was on the student. The Jews cherished the Torah, and still do. This was evident in the time of King Josiah (1 Kings 22:1–13). The Jews thought that if one generation neglected the Torah, the book of the Law, the nation was doomed. They desired to maintain the integrity of the Torah, and uphold its role in the lives of the Jewish people. The Torah was the centre of education, and from it came every aspect of learning. It was the very core of Jewish religious and secular culture.

History indicates that rabbis would select boys as young as five years of age for training to become future rabbis. Young boys could also ask a rabbi if they might follow him and be discipled. This was a privileged opportunity not easily obtained. In modern day Judaism, what the student is majoring in is not paramount; the student's commitment to Judaism, his rabbinical qualifications, and his character are foremost.

A question might be raised here. How would the character of so young a potential student be determined? On the basis of common sense, this would be done by observation, coming out of a close and observant relationship. This observation would not only be in the classroom, but in the daily activities of life, leading to a firm sense of discipleship.

Matthew 8:19 shows that it was an honour to be allowed to follow a rabbi, and that following brought expectations: "*Then a certain scribe came and said to Him, 'Teacher, I will follow you wherever you go.'*" According to Jesus's response, the individual who said this had not considered the cost of following Him, and therefore did not qualify. The honour of following a spiritual leader was practiced by those who followed pastors in early American and Canadian church history. However, it appears to have been lost in the functioning of the church today. There are many pastors who wish to be "one of the boys" with members of their congregations, and thereby lose that position of honour and respect. They tend perhaps to minimize their role as instructors and examples. We need those who will instead set a pattern as they lead and teach in constructive and productive ways.

In Matthew 9:9 there is an instance of Jesus asking a man to follow Him:

> *As Jesus passed on from there, He saw a man named Matthew sitting at the tax table. And He said to him, 'Follow Me.' So he arose and followed Him.*

The intriguing part of this passage is that Jesus asks this of a man who would have been much despised: a hated tax collector for the Romans. As a customs officer, Matthew would be seen to be one of the most unlikely men to be offered the privilege and honour of following Christ. Tax collectors were branded with "*sinners*" (Matthew 9:11). They were considered unpatriotic and exposed to ritual uncleanness. Matthew would be considered as a traitor to Israel and desiring his own benefit. Societally he and others in his line of work would be seen as occupying the bottom of the barrel.

Jesus actually went to the home of Matthew (also known as Levi, as indicated in Mark 2:15–17 and Luke 5:29). Sitting at a meal with Matthew would be a sign of intimacy, of acceptance, of commitment to Him. When Jesus called Matthew to follow him, He was calling an outcast to a position of honour. The point was no longer who Matthew was, but that Jesus called people to follow Him for a purpose. He called men whom He considered trainable and useable. Jesus saw potential in Matthew—which is what a discipler will do—and He worked to develop that potential.

Today's culture of hurry works against the process of developing potential; we need to stand against this aspect of the prevailing culture in order to develop men and women to serve in the Kingdom. Jesus demonstrated the proven method of selecting people with the right qualities and training them according to their personalities and strengths. A return to that kind of discipleship is essential in order to maintain the centrality and integrity of Scripture. Consider the two members of the American military and one civilian who disabled a terrorist on a train in France in 2014. One might ask why they acted as they did. The answer lies in the preparedness of two of the three men. They were trained to recognize the sounds of an AK–47 being readied for action, and they responded to it instinctively. That kind of assessment and readiness for action will be needed to produce men and women of spiritual character.

A similar idea occurs in 2 Timothy 2:2, where Timothy is instructed to teach men who will be able to teach others also. Discipleship will provide the best opportunity for that type of training; we need to help others begin to move toward that conviction. A generational move back in that direction needs to be pursued with conviction because it will require generations. The road back must begin somewhere, and the best place and time is here and now.

Chapter Three

DISCIPLESHIP AS A LIFESTYLE

Discipleship is not an add-on or a gifting entrusted to a few people, but is an obligation to the church in its entirety. Each follower of Christ needs to be burdened for others to the point where each one will wish to disciple someone in their growth in Christ.

When asking professing followers of Christ to identify how God is transforming them, the answer will reveal much about their theology, or lack thereof. Many might say, or think they should say, that God had at some point "zapped" them in some way, and that transformation had happened. What the transformation looks like may be difficult to describe. Transformation is the process of growing in the knowledge of Scripture, and in intimacy with Jesus Christ, leading to a life of increasing holiness. In many cases people believe that transformation has been, or should have been, instantaneous. This may well be the consequence of living in our culture of instant gratification. However, a study of Jesus's work with His disciples should be ample evidence that such change does not take place instantaneously. Rather it took place over a period of three years with a lot of interaction, communication, and accountability.

Observe the conduct of people at a vending machine who pay for something and do not get what they wanted, or do not get it instantly. You will see reflected an instant gratification culture. Some will respond with unpleasant comments, or a kick to the vending machine. Similarly, we are impatient with any process of spiritual development, often bypassing such a process because it doesn't have instant results and instead requires effort.

During my visit to the Dominican Republic in 1987 I was reminded of this point while observing the gentleman in charge of showing the *Jesus* film. He led the prayer for the group who remained behind after viewing the film. It would appear that evangelists had often prayed for (or perhaps preyed upon) these same people. The demanding nature of their prayers and the volume of the voices during the prayers, indicated that they expected and even required an immediate answer. It reminded me of the prophets of Baal (1 Kings 18:25–29) whose lengthy, loud prayers did not produce the desired result. Of course, they did not know they were crying out to a non-existent entity, so they were expecting immediate results. We are praying to a patient, purposeful, real God, and so we are to be content with His timing in His answers.

A newborn child is not expected to display instant growth and maturity. Our expectation should be no different in the development of a newborn child of God. The infant believer must be nurtured, with appropriate expectations, patience, and consistency. Spiritual development requires patience and endurance, a reminder of the qualities mentioned in Galatians 5:22–23a: "*But the fruit of the Spirit is love, joy, peace, longsuffering, kindness, goodness, faithfulness, gentleness, self-control.*" These qualities are a requirement in the life of the developing follower of Christ, and on the part of the one who is discipling others. The process must of necessity develop into a lifestyle where patience is practised.

In our modern church, spiritual development is expected to be instantaneous. This may be why many who profess to believe are discouraged in following Christ when their growth falls short of their unrealistic expectations. The *"longsuffering"* of Galatians 5:22 comes into play in this process of spiritual formation. We need to practise a lifestyle of discipleship where we minister to each other as we grow in our walk with Christ.

Spiritual formation, as used here, is the process of learning about Christ, and seeing the necessity of growth in the principles that will cause one to become more and more Christ-like. As this necessity sinks in, the individual will seek and practice the disciplines that will bring about the desired change in character.

In the process of seeking spiritual formation there is a danger of what is called "works righteousness." This view is to appropriate the gospel on the action side of life, where the focus is on doing rather than on being.

It is beneficial to look at the difference between the nature of humanity and the actions of humanity in understanding what is required to produce a life of righteousness. I have found an illustration called the Sin Continuum to be very helpful. It looks like this.

Sin (outward)	Sin (nature)
Committed	Nature
Outward	Inward
Doing	Being

The very basic question here is: where on the Sin Continuum should the process of discipleship begin? If we focus on the left column, we have people who obey rules because they are told to. On the right are people who obey commands out of reverence for God who has given the commands. The focus on the right will be based on a genuine change brought about by the work of the Spirit of God.

But should people be told to stop sinning in order to be better? Or do we help people become stronger in their faith, so they may stop sinning? At what point on the Sin Continuum is the gospel appropriated? Is it on the side of being or doing? Here is where what theologian Dietrich Bonhoeffer called "cheap grace" is employed.[9] Cheap grace excuses sin rather than requiring repentance. We have been told that our problem is not sin, but merely bad habits. This is where starting on the doing side becomes very popular, because repentance and forgiveness

---

9   Dietrich Bonhoeffer, *The Cost of Discipleship,* Simon and Shuster, New York, NY, 1959, p.43

are not essential. Bonhoeffer says cheap grace means the justification of sin rather than the justification of the sinner. Cheap grace has little or no expectation or requirement. Little thought is given to the consequences of sin. Cheap grace simply wipes out sin and makes the individual's world acceptable. It excuses rather than holding accountable; it does not demand obedience. It justifies sin, not the sinner. Steve Gallagher has contributed another definition of cheap grace: "Weak conversion and a compromising lifestyle."[10] This theology has far-reaching consequences and should be carefully evaluated. Professor Richard Foster adds a helpful statement: "Sinful practices become their habits, then their choices, and finally their character."[11] The best way of avoiding this is to practice intentional discipleship based on a genuine conversion experience and to practice ongoing growth in a change of character.

Some may remember the phenomenon of asking the question, What Would Jesus Do? with its WWJD buttons and wristbands. The question would be better stated "What would Jesus have me do?" This moves the issue from the theoretical to the practical. When stated this way, the onus falls on our obedience to Christ. Obedience and accountability must be two major components of a discipling relationship. Professor and

---

10 Steve Gallagher, *Intoxicated with Babylon*, Pure Life Ministries, Dry Ridge, KY, 2007, p.36

11 Richard Foster, *The Celebration of Discipline*, Harper Collins, New York, NY, 1978, p.83

philosopher Dallas Willard makes a useful statement: "Spiritual formation must begin on the sin nature side. It is a matter of re-forming the broken soul of man in a recovery from its alienation from God."[12]

The concept of repenting of sin and forsaking sin is beauti-fully stated by Jesus in His instruction to the adulterous woman: "*...go and sin no more*" (John 8:11).

One question to ponder on this issue is whether discipleship focuses on the new birth, or on sin management. Some churches have displayed the culture of trying to manage *conduct*. There is danger in giving an individual a false sense of assurance. Pas-tor and author Peter Scazzero was having a seemingly successful ministry when he began to be at odds with himself in living a life in Christ. When his marriage came to a crisis point, he and his wife carefully evaluated their life and ministry. They concluded they were busy focusing on doing and therefore had neglected understanding who they were in Christ. He said they then went from being "human doings" to human beings. He added that "I labored at serving people, forgiving people, humbling myself, and being joyful," in relation to doing rather than operating out of the interior of being. Scazzero and his wife went from the left side of the Sin Continuum to the right.[13]

---

12 Dallas Willard, *The Great Omission,* Monarch Books, Oxford U.K. 2006, p.156

13 Peter Scazzero, *The Emotionally Healthy Church,* Zondervan, Grand Rapids, Mich. 2003, p.34

Author Robert Mulholland contributes to this discussion: "Repentance is not being sorry for what we have done; it is being sorry for being a person who would do such things."[14]

Dallas Willard makes a perceptive statement: "Spiritual formation refers to the process of shaping our spirit and giving it a definite character. It means the formation of our spirit in conformity with the Spirit of Christ."[15]

The foremost goal of discipleship is that "...*Christ is formed in you*" (Galatians 4:19). Spiritual formation does not aim to control actions, nor make behaviour modification, but instead seeks that every believer be formed by the image of Christ. Focus on action alone takes us into social conformity, the deadliest of legalisms. Spiritual formation reworks all aspects of the human being: heart, mind, will, body, social relations. None of these are independent of each other.

Having come to spiritual formation on the right side of the Sin Continuum, we now move to the left side where the transformed nature springs into action in the living out of life. Character is formed through action and is transformed through action, as we can see in Romans 12:2. These actions include carefully planned and grace-sustained disciplines that have results. Matthew 7:16–20 speaks to this principle of results by

---

14 Robert Mulholland Jr., *Invitation to a Journey,* InterVarsity Press, Prospect Heights, Ill. 1993, p.23

15 Dallas Willard, *The Great Omission,* Monarch Books, Oxford U.K. 2006, p.53

using the image of a fruit-bearing tree. If we tend to the tree, the fruit will take care of itself. This is where discipleship is so valuable a ministry, just as trees require nurture. The discipler cannot manufacture fruit; it is the product of the work of the Holy Spirit in the life of the one who is committed to following Christ. John 15 is a good reference for this discussion as it shows our need for abiding in Christ in order to bear fruit. Further, the discussion on the lifestyle of discipleship which is based on Jesus's last command to the twelve apostles (Matthew 28:16–20), will follow in the next chapter.

Let's give consideration to a few more thoughts about discipleship. Discipleship is supported by the teaching of the Apostle Paul who wrote to those who heard the gospel from him, "*Therefore I urge you, imitate me*" (1 Corinthians 4:16). He was not hesitant to encourage them to imitate him, which is an honourable ambition in discipleship. He says this also in 1 Corinthians 11:1, "*Imitate me, just as I also imitate Christ*" and in Philippians 3:17, "*Brethren, join in following my example, and note those who so walk, as you have us for a pattern.*" Hebrews 6:12 also speaks to the principle of following a pattern set before us, encouraging the believers "*that you do not become sluggish, but imitate those who through faith and patience inherit the promises.*" The repetition of these statements points to the importance Scripture places on imitation.

In visiting and observing churches, it has been evident that some are clearly over-programmed. Due to the number of volunteers and amount of time required to run these programs, there is no time for developing relationships. A significant hindrance to meaningful relationships is the sense that "one-size-fits-all." Programs are designed in a way that is meant to have the same value to all participants. The sense is that if a program worked for one, it must work for others as well. It is felt that if the program does not work, it must be the learner's fault. But discipleship, on the other hand, speaks to the needs of the individual. Each individual has unique needs, needs that the program manuals may not touch on at all.

I do not care for discipleship books, unless they are purely philosophical in content, offering a general understanding of the principles involved in making discipleship effective.

Discipleship needs to be tailored to the one being discipled. It will take time to get to know the individual's personality, background, gifts, talents and aspirations. In discipleship, we help the disciple seek and find his or her dream. In church ministries or any large group meetings it is easy for people to lose interest because what is being taught does not speak to their individual need at the moment. Discipleship allows the focus to be on the needs and challenges of the individual disciple. This is where one-on-one discipleship may have an advantage over small group discipleship, although both have great benefit.

The temptation is to disciple in such a manner that the discipler is in control of the schedule and the topic. But this rigid schedule makes discipleship a program if the individual's needs are overlooked. One must *listen* to the disciple in order to hear the practical needs of the disciple and to begin to respond to those needs. A discipler may have an outline of proposed topics to discuss and a schedule that will determine perceived success, but the schedule must take second place to the immediate issues expressed.

In my first position as assistant pastor I was carefully discipled by the senior pastor. We met weekly to study Moses's leadership style. My senior pastor used this opportunity to guide me in strengthening my gift of leadership, along with preaching and teaching. He was careful to make the training applicable to my personality and gifting. That is the strength of intentional discipleship. Programs may contain all kinds of busyness but they cannot hold a candle to discipleship in terms of productivity.

Discipleship is a process of learning and doing. A discipler needs to know if a disciple is committed to this process rather than simply a short-term program. One needs to determine if the candidate for discipleship is willing and committed, so that time and energy is not spent on someone who is not willing to obey Scripture. This is not harshness, but solid reality. Consider the disciples who forsook Jesus: *From that time many of His disciples went back and walked with Him no more*" (John 6:66). There is no record of Him cajoling them to reconsider; He fully accepted their choice to abandon Him. In fact, he offered the Twelve the opportunity to leave as well. Thus the commitment to discipleship ministry must be made by both parties.

I told one disciple that the difference between him and me was that he looked for fault, while I looked for potential. In the discipleship process, we seek to help a person meet that potential. This is not to discourage the process of holding Bible studies, but we should turn the sessions into accountability groups. Many people want Bible studies, but not discipleship, because they do not want to be held accountable.

We must be committed to the process in spite of the challenges, even when the progress may not be evident to anyone else for a period of time. On this matter, there is a statement attributed to the seventeenth century spiritual writer Francis Fenelon: "God hides His work, in the spiritual order as in the natural, under an unnoticeable sequence of events."[16]

---

16 Source unknown

Chapter Four

DISCIPLESHIP JESUS-STYLE

CONSTRUCTION ON GERMANY'S COLOGNE CATHEDRAL BEGAN IN 1248 and was halted in 1473, leaving it unfinished. Work restarted in the 19th century and was completed, according to the original plan, in 1880. Cologne's medieval builders had planned a grand structure to house the reliquary of the Three Kings and fit its role as a place of worship for the Roman emperors. Despite having been left incomplete during the medieval period, Cologne Cathedral eventually became unified as "a masterpiece of exceptional intrinsic value" and "a powerful testimony to the strength and persistence of religious belief in medieval and modern Europe."[17] Those who laboured on it over the 632 years of its construction knew they would never see its completion. A firm commitment to their objective was required.

Contrast that project with the modern approach of business, as seen in a major food chain.

---

17 Michael Horton, *Ordinary*, Zondervan, Grand Rapids, Mich. 2014, p.32

McDonald's brand mission is to be our customers' favorite place and way to eat and drink. Our world-wide operations are aligned around a global strategy called the Plan to Win, which centers on an exceptional customer experience—People, Product, Place, Price and Promotion. We are committed to continuously improving our operations and enhancing our customers' experience.[18]

Because the bottom line in business is profit, the goals must be of an immediate nature: pleasing people in the present.

The immediate-gain objective of McDonald's is often the goal of the modern church. There is a misunderstood emphasis on relevance, with the church primarily concerned about being relevant to culture, just as McDonald's desire is to be relevant to society. In this mistaken process the church has become conformed to the world. This practice is spoken against in Romans 12:2 which says,

And do not be conformed to this world, but be transformed by the renewing of your mind, that you may prove what is that good and acceptable and perfect will of God.

I believe it is profitable to examine discipleship objectives from two perspectives. The first is found in 2 Timothy 2:2

---

18 Ibid, p.32

which says, "*And the things you have heard me say in the presence of many witnesses entrust to reliable people who will also be qualified to teach others.*" This passage shows how discipleship is built generation upon generation in contrast to those who seek to see the fruit of labour in one generation. To determine biblically which approach is better, I would like to offer a more thorough discussion on Matthew 28:18–20, Jesus's Great Commission.

There are four clearly stated parts in the Great Commission. We need to examine each of these four to regulate our understanding of discipleship:

Go

Notice that Jesus did not say *come*. This is not a passive command. God did not give us a theory to ponder, but a command to go, even as He did when He sent Jesus Christ into the world. We are to go find people needing ministry in their lives. In this context discipleship is intentional, purposeful, and measurable. (As a side-note, preaching can be intentional and purposeful, but it may fall short in measurable results.) Going to where the followers of Christ are to help them into a deeper walk with Christ means we will also go to the people in the world who need to hear about the possibility and the blessing of a walk with Christ.

This was illustrated by my relationship with a shop supervisor who was my boss for two years. Because he knew of my faith in Christ, from my resume as well as from observation as we worked together, we had many chats regarding the Christian faith. I fully respected the time I was paid for, so I went to his office at his invitation. He responded to the biblical message based on our relationship. I contend that is a most effective way to reach people for Christ. This type of ministry has discipleship built into it, so it is more effective. The whole family came to know the Lord after I left that place of employment, and he and I remained good friends. Thus I conclude that an understanding and application of discipleship will lead to evangelism, which demands further discipleship.

The modern method of planting churches in North America follows common patterns: train the finest of preachers; arrange for excellent musicians; secure a fairly attractive place of meeting; print and distribute slick and colourful announcements inviting people in the community to come to attend the meetings or participate in the planned programs. We say "come" and feel people are being reached. But Jesus said "go."

If Jesus's command had said to come, God could well have strung a large banner across the sky by some means, announcing the coming of Jesus Christ, and inviting people to come. God told His Son to go, and Jesus passed on the same command to the church. If we were to tell others to come, the task of the church might be to disinfect Christians by isolating them and teaching them to do good deeds. But discipleship means propelling followers of Christ into the world to risk their lives for others for Jesus's sake. The essence of the command to "go" is to share life with learners on the basis of relationship.

Make disciples

To make disciples means to intentionally draw alongside another person with the purpose of building up his or her life, nurturing that life to a measure of maturity. Dallas Willard has done the church a great service by drawing attention to the omission of the discipling part of the Great Commission, in his book *The Great Omission*.

When discipleship is omitted there is a tendency to at least lessen the practice of "*teaching them to observe all things that I have commanded you*" (Matthew 28:20). Let the professionals to do the teaching, people may say. After all, that is what they are paid to do!

By contrast, observe what Jesus actually did during His time on earth. There is little indication of what He did until He was about thirty years of age, but for the following three years there is a full description of His activities. John 17:4 gives clear insights into His work before He was crucified. He said, "...*I have finished the work which You have given me to do*." What is the work He has finished? Many commentaries on the Gospel of John make no reference to verse 4. Some refer to the statement to mean that the work referred to was as good as done: providing salvation on the Cross. But that work was not yet done. It was later, on the Cross, that He said, "*It is finished*" (John 19:30).

Pastor Mark Johnson says,

The greatest demonstration of the Son's love was when He 'finished the work' His Father gave Him (17:4). This statement anticipated the next day on the

Cross, when He cried 'it is finished', signaling that our sins were paid in full (19:30).[19]

Others say that He has completed the work "in His will," which is basically a restatement of the aforementioned, but I feel we must reject that interpretation.

The Bible Exposition Commentary comes closest to what the text actually says with the following words, "this work included His messages and miracles on earth and the training of the twelve for future service."

We know in John 13–17 that Jesus is with the disciples at what is known as the Last Supper. Until the end of chapter 17, almost all of what is recorded is His direct teaching of the twelve disciples. In chapter 17, He prays for and about the twelve disciples. His last three years had been spent emphasizing the training of the Twelve. If the work He referred to had been only to give His life on the Cross, He could have come down and spent about four days on earth to accomplish it.

The three years of Jesus's ministry are significant due to the discipleship training of those who would take the gospel throughout the world. The Twelve are the focus of His prayer in chapter 17, which in verse 20 He expands to those who, in the future, will believe. The task of carrying on His ministry is left to those He has trained by discipleship. They are the ones who in

---

19 Mark Johnson, *Israel My Glory,* November/December 2016, Bellmawr, NJ, p.22

the book of Acts are involved in the founding and the explosive growth of the church. I believe the work He refers to here is that of the essential training of the twelve apostles.

The leadership in the local church, then, needs to follow that principle of training, and to disciple those who will carry on the work after them. This is an effective way to see the work of reaching a lost world continue to function.

Baptize them

Baptism ought to be seen as a vital part of the nurturing process of the church. It needs to be taught as an act of identification with Christ in His burial and resurrection, and with the Body of Christ. It is also to be observed in recognition of the three Persons of the Godhead. Understood in those terms, baptism speaks to the fellowship which gives blessing and the opportunity to be a blessing. Ephesians 4 and Acts 2 speak in a marvelous way to the beauty and effectiveness of the fellowship that should exist.

Teach them to obey

Teaching Scripture is both a great privilege and responsibility. James 3:1 cautions, "*My brethren, let not many of you become teachers, knowing that we shall receive a stricter judgment.*" Teaching not only involves Scripture, but also discussing matters of living the Christian life to the fullest. Let me illustrate the value of general teaching with a personal story. In 1954 we were building a new barn on the family farm to replace one that had been dismantled after a major windstorm had severely damaged it. I was thirteen years of age, and not very adept with tools. I was on the roof with a few others to assist with the task of shingling. One gentleman saw me swinging the hammer in an awkward manner. It could have been an excellent opportunity to teach me how to swing it properly, but he chose instead to ridicule me. He and I both missed out on the opportunity of a teachable moment.

In the process of making disciples, we must teach for the purpose of producing a humble spirit of obedience to the teachings of Scripture. This has the potential of producing a growing holiness in the life of the disciple. One does not accidentally become holy. It is not something we drift into. The process of becoming like Christ requires passionate, well-informed action on our part. Discipleship has the objective of teaching the disciples to obey "...*all things that I have commanded you*" (Matthew 28:20). This is supported by the words of Joshua 1:8,

> *This Book of the Law shall not depart from your mouth, but you shall meditate in it day and night, that you may observe to do according to all that is written in it.*

This involves more than teaching, but must necessarily involve accountability and correction, as indicated in 2 Timothy 3:16–17:

> *All Scripture is given by inspiration of God, and is profitable for doctrine, for reproof, for correction, for instruction in righteousness, that the man of God may be complete, thoroughly equipped for every good work.*

This is supported by the Apostle Paul's words that we are to be *"teaching and admonishing one another"* (Colossians 3:16). "Admonish" is a significant word meaning to "caution or reprove gently."[20] That requires accountability to one another to be effective.

There are serious misconceptions about the nature of accountability that might be confusing. Accountability could be seen as a church holding members accountable for certain actions or code of conduct, or confessing sins to one another, as it says in James 5:16. That is not the sole emphasis here. We will consider accountability as believers holding each other accountable for the disciplines that will produce ongoing spiritual growth in the knowledge of God and in the biblical practices of holy living. In this scenario, believers challenge each other in terms of time spent in Scripture reading and in meditation on what excites them from a specific text on any given day. The challenges to obey the Word would come out of such interactions.

At age twenty-one, I once stood in the lunch line at a Bible institute with one of the professors of the school. He engaged me in discussion on the church service I had attended the previous day. Having answered that I had enjoyed the sermon, he then asked me what text the sermon was based on. That was one of the most embarrassing experiences of my life for I could not remember. Although I was in the process of preparing for some sort of Bible ministry, his question revealed to my lack of disciplined learning. He took it upon himself to hold me accountable

---

for one of the simple disciplines of the Christian faith, that of paying attention to the Word of God. This is the kind of caring and interaction that defines accountability in the ministry of discipleship and nurture. His words taught and encouraged me as a brother in the pursuit of excellence.

Discipleship is an intentional teaching process with the measurable goal of greater holiness. Believers should be known for raising the bar, not accepting the status quo. We should not fear raising the bar for others, even as we do so for ourselves.

John 6 demonstrates in part the process of discipleship that Jesus held to. This passage goes against the idea of people trying to find their inner self. Frankly, while finding the inner self is the pursuit of psychotherapy, we also need to recall, as Jeremiah 17:9 says, *"The heart is deceitful above all things, and desperately wicked; who can know it?"* The inner self will seek to justify the imaginations and actions of the unregenerate person. The Christian must seek truth outside of themselves. Thus Jesus pointed to Himself as the truth (John 14:6). Jesus's teaching in chapter 6 as in chapter 14 is not popular today, either in society or in church. It receives a strong reaction today, as it did in His day, when many of His disciples *"went back and walked with Him no more'* (John 6:66). To *"walk with Him no more"* sounds tragically permanent. They completely disassociated with His teaching in this chapter and Jesus allowed them to do so.

When we risk losing numbers in church attendance, we often ask: "How can we bring these people back?" or "How can we adjust our teaching so people will not leave?"

These were not questions that appear to have crossed Jesus's mind. In fact, He did not even try to fortify the remaining Twelve. He gave them the opportunity to leave, too. The majority of those who were following Him believed intellectually but were not ready to make a heart commitment. Jesus, however, wanted and wants disciples who are fully committed.

Discipling others requires a full commitment on the part of both. Those who walked away were reacting negatively to the truth he taught. This means a rejection of Him because He is Truth (John 14:6). A discipler cannot say to anyone that they themselves are the Truth, but we do represent and present the Truth. Peter's response in John 6:68 indicates that the Twelve understood that a commitment to Him was the only profitable way. I say the Twelve, but it is apparent that Judas did not accept the idea of commitment to truth, so it turned out to be eleven.

This commitment to truth is sadly lacking today. The tendency is to make Jesus soft, gentle, and patronizing, at the expense of commitment. Former U.S. President Obama, in response to the Supreme Court decision approving of same-sex marriage, said in a White House statement in 2016, "Our Union has just become a little more perfect." This indicates how far Western society, and Western churches have strayed from truth. I say Western churches because many churches have bought into the same philosophy expressed by President Obama.

The discipler must guide disciples to Jesus Christ, and to Scripture. Colossians 3:5 states that covetousness is idolatrous. Coveting a lifestyle that is contrary to Scripture makes us guilty of idolatry. That means we are worshiping something other than God. Our lifestyle, building, and programs may well be idols among churchgoing people. Jesus had diligently discipled the Twelve and when He ascended to heaven He left only 120 faithful followers. By today's standards He would be considered a dismal failure. Yet Acts 2 declares what an impact these people had on the growth of the church.

Chapter Five

DISCIPLESHIP AND ITS OBJECTIVE

EPHESIANS 4:11–14 GIVES US A GOOD DESCRIPTION OF WHAT GOD wants to see evident in the believer's life: maturity, stability, and an obedient faith. In the process of this development, He wants to equip the saints for the work of ministry. This passage provides a clear and detailed statement about the objective of discipleship.

The principle of discipleship will be a question of finding the treasure that is hidden behind the outward expression of the child of God. The treasure that needs to be discovered may well be a walk with God that encourages the church. Or it may be a giftedness that will only be revealed through ongoing discipleship, and demonstrated by the discipled Christian confidently serving in the name of the Lord. We don't know what is hidden behind the exterior of those who we wish would show a greater demonstration of love for and commitment to the Lord. We may not be able to comprehend any beauty in that individual until we pour our lives into that life and begin to see that beauty emerge.

Pastor Mark Buchanan tells of a riverside park in Guelph, Ontario, which gets drained by the city each spring so that its citizens can clean up the debris from the river bottom and its banks. The city then calls together sculptors to make works of art using only the debris. The sculptures are showcased in the park along the river.[21]

In like manner, discipleship should be seen as taking something that's perhaps unlovely and transforming it into something beautiful. A nurturing context is required with each member of the Body of Christ looking for what he or she can do to make a positive difference. A very dear friend of mine who suffered with ALS had a statement emblazoned on one of his shirts that read, "Have you made a difference today?" This attitude reflects the spirit that should be a driving force in the life of a restored Child of God.

In *The Cost of Discipleship,* Dietrich Bonhoeffer[22] asserts that it is a single step to have faith and be obedient. Such an assertion may be difficult to accept in today's culture (and possibly even in church culture) which treats a person's right to make individual choices as non-negotiable. This idea runs counters to authentic Christian discipleship. To embrace God's will, we will need to undergo a massive change in culture.

In John 14:21 Jesus states in no uncertain terms:

---

21 Mark Buchanan, *The Rest of God: Restoring your soul by restoring Sabbath,* Thomas Nelson, Nashville, TN. 2006, p.68

22 Dietrich Bonhoeffer, *The Cost of Discipleship*, Simon and Shuster, New York, NY, 1959, pp.63-69

He who has my commandments and keeps them, it is he who loves me. And he who loves me will be loved by My Father, and I will love him and manifest myself to him.

When faced with such an assertion, we can respond with a classic demonstration of how widespread the practice of deifying personal choices has become. Someone may object, "I don't want all these rules; I just want to follow Jesus." What such a person is truly saying is that they want to love Jesus, but don't want to obey Him. This is an example of claiming the right of choice. But concerning Christ, one cannot pick and choose. Our duty is to follow Him. It is not a request or a suggestion; it is a command. Can we love Jesus without obeying Him? We perceive this to be an option. We pride ourselves on the basis of being able to make a choice. But you don't get to choose. You get to follow.

In biblical times, people made choices. The Apostle Paul speaks directly to some in I Corinthians 3:1–4, calling them carnal:

And I, brethren, could not speak to you as to spiritual people but as to carnal, as to babes in Christ. I fed you with milk and not with solid food; for until now you were not able to receive it, and even now you are still not able; for you are still carnal. For where there are envy, strife, and divisions among you, are you not carnal and behaving like mere men? For when one says, "I am of Paul," and another, "I am of Apollos," are you not carnal?

49

According to the Bible the only choice is whether to follow. We cannot choose to love Jesus and not follow Him.

I've met people who believe that Jesus Christ has set them free from obedience to His commands because obeying commands means legalism. This is based on a false understanding of John 8:36 (*"Therefore if the Son makes you free, you shall be free indeed"*) where freedom is falsely seen as the opportunity to please oneself. Before becoming people of faith, we were free to go our own way, but Christ has set us free to go His way. We have not been set free from His commands, but rather set free to obey His commands.

Bonhoeffer poses some interesting questions in this regard. "Is obedience subsequent to faith? Does faith exist without obedience?"[23] Let's return to the objective of discipleship, which Ephesians 4:12–14 says is maturity and stability. Those qualities develop through following Him and walking in His way. Our secular understanding of personal choices has badly distorted our concept of faith. Do we *need* options? No, we *want* options that will enhance our lifestyles. Taking a look at the automobile or any other industry reveals to us the incredible pull of personal choice: they design and incorporate into their products a huge number of options in order to appeal to a wide range of customers. Jesus didn't promote options for us; He gave us commands to obey.[24] We ask, "What do people want?" But we should be

---

23 Ibid, ch.2

24 David Platt, *Radical,* Multnomah, Colorado Springs, Colorado, 2010, p.121

asking, "What do people need?" Why do people lay claim to faith, but choose to walk in disobedience? They do so simply for the love of options from which they can make the best choices, as they see it. But Bonhoeffer makes the point, with conviction, that faith is only real when there is obedience. When Peter, in Matthew 14 steps out of the boat at Jesus's urging, he is acting in unconditional obedience. In Luke 9:57–62 the three who encounter Jesus try to set conditions for following Him. But Jesus rejects this. This becomes a program to suit our desires, based on rationality.[25] Here is a statement by Bonhoeffer that deserves our attention: "Only those who believe are obedient, and only those who are obedient believe."[26] To illustrate: I once had lunch with my son and two of his friends, one of whom claimed a strong faith. He made the comment that he believed that, with the indwelling Holy Spirit, he had the assurance that when he met a person in a wheelchair, he could speak healing to that individual, and it would be done. Then he made the comment that negated what he had just said. He told us he felt guilty every time he walked by a person in a wheelchair and he did not speak words of healing. I would hope that if I believed in my gifting of healing I would go out looking for people in wheelchairs! In discipleship we try to move people from this dichotomy of faith and obedience to a biblical unity of the two.

---

25 Dietrich Bonhoeffer, *The Cost of Discipleship,* Simon and Shuster, New York, NY, 1959, p.61

26 Ibid, p.63

During most of my pastoral years, I preached twice each Sunday, taught an adult Bible class and taught Bible at the Wednesday prayer meeting. With that teaching commitment, I felt I really could not effectively disciple people to the point where they would make a choice to obey what the Scriptures teach. It is true there are those individuals with a measure of maturity who can and will translate truth into practice but for many people this requires a process of discipleship. Teaching generally provides knowledge, but obedience comes through discipleship, along with the qualities of accountability and observation of lifestyle. One-on-one or small group intentional discipleship will be more effective in this process of teaching and learning. Pastor and author Greg Ogden says that a significant portion of a leader's time should be given to a chosen few who will carry on the work after he or she is gone; this means having enough vision to think small.

1 Timothy 4:12 speaks to the essential nature of example: "*Let no one despise your youth, but be an example to the believers in word, in conduct, in love, in spirit, in faith, in purity.*" The best examples come from those believers who show maturity and stability. It is in immaturity that apostasy sets in (Hebrews 5:12–6:1).

The Apostle Paul addresses this theme in 2 Thessalonians 3:9 in the context of giving himself to ministry to others: "… *not because we do not have authority, but to make ourselves an example of how you should follow us.*" He urges believers to follow his example, which leads to the conclusion that believers are to be conscious of needing to be an example.

Teaching and example are both essential elements of the building of a good foundation. I am reminded of a work experience I had in my early twenties. I worked for the summer on a construction site of a science building at a university in Winnipeg. I had just spent six months in school, and was not prepared for the type of work required. The excavation was four metres deep, and in it were trenches another metre deep. It was in these trenches that we were digging holes a metre across and a metre deep. The temperature was thirty-one degrees Celsius on a day when I was working in a place that hardly anyone would see. The temptation could have been strong to cut corners but the purpose of the project was to build the foundation of a large structure.

In the same way we must do the unnoticed work of building a foundation in the lives of individuals, knowing that what is built on that foundation will be noticed. In discipleship ministry, be prepared to do the essential work that may never be noticed. That foundation is hard to construct if individuals are only involved in attending services and Sunday school. The information they receive is very valuable, but they also need help in applying what they have learned.

Dr. Albert Mohler tells of growing up in a part of the state of Florida, in which there are two particular snakes, the coral snake and the scarlet king. The coral snake is highly toxic, and the scarlet king is safe enough to be anyone's pet. They are very similar in size and color, both having red, black, and yellow stripes. One needs information to tell them apart in order to avoid the coral snake. In order to do so, Dr. Mohler learned a poem which said, in part, "Red and yellow, kill a fellow; red and black, a friend of Jack." On the coral snake the red and yellow stripes touch, while on the scarlet king the red and black stripes touch. That information helped him and others be safe. Similarly, correct biblical information is essential to avoiding apostasy. One does not drift into a state of holiness. However, one can drift into apostasy by neglect or ignorance of right information. There needs to be a passion for the sharing of the correct biblical knowledge.

The Reformers, such as Luther, Calvin, and Knox, taught the Catechism to the youth of the local churches. They did not simply disseminate information, but helped the youth see the application of that information. Even in their time, the Reformers saw the need for the Catechism as a means of discipleship.

One objective of discipleship is preparation for persecution. This concept comes from Bonhoeffer who suffered severe persecution for righteousness. Matthew 5:10 tells us that those who are persecuted for righteousness are blessed. If we are persecuted, it ought to be for righteousness and just judgment, and not for our own foolishness or bad behaviour. The believer's righteousness will be offensive to the world, but we won't be persecuted for being nice and accommodating in order to avoid being disliked for a walk of righteousness.

Bonhoeffer says not to resist the evil that imposes suffering on the follower of Christ for righteousness.[27] The intent of evil

---

27 Dietrich Bonhoeffer, *A Testament to Freedom,* Edited by Geffrey B. Kelly and F. Burton Nelson, Harper One, New York, NY, 1990, p.317

is to breed further evil. When we patiently endure suffering, we take away its sting. When we proclaim righteousness and justice, we are not resisting but are offering an alternative. Bonhoeffer was a man who lived in the presence of persecution; it was not theoretical to him. Persecution is to be an expected part of righteousness.

If a man sues a believer for his coat, he is to give him his cloak as well, and if one compels a believer to carry his burden one mile, he is to carry it two miles (Matthew 5:41). That is not resistance to evil; it is overcoming evil by good deeds and attitude.

A disciple is not prepared for persecution by theology alone. He or she will be prepared by nurturing the soul through discipleship and by helping the disciple to understand something of the passion of the Cross. It needs to become significant to the disciple that the Cross is an expression of passion. The Cross was the crucial act in the life of Christ. So His follower must walk in total willingness to bear his cross. As Jesus said, "*If any one desires to come after Me, let him deny himself, and take up his cross daily, and follow me*" (Luke 9:23). To bear our cross is not an accident; it is the fruit of obedience and exclusive allegiance to Jesus Christ.

Chapter Six

DISCIPLESHIP WILL CHANGE A CULTURE

THE AMERICAN DREAM WAS A DREAM OF A LAND IN WHICH LIFE should be better and wider and fuller for everyone, with opportunity for each according to ability or achievement. It was a dream that spurred on westward expansion of the United States.

This dream can be used to define today's secular culture as well as church culture. It has become a culture of entitlement with the mentality that government owes me, the church owes me, and easily shifts into the belief that God owes me.

From observation, reading, and discussion I have concluded that the church has also fallen into the error of entitlement, and perhaps to a greater degree than society in general. The tragedy is that the focus of the church, too often, is on what I can get out of it. Nations try to change the culture of other nations. For example: Russia, the United States, and Canada have tried to change the culture of Afghanistan, and there is ample evidence that forcing such change on a national level is not successful. The church, however, must work at changing its own culture in order to become biblically meaningful and effective.

A culture is a pattern of learned behaviour, practised by a society, which has developed over generations. "Culture is the anthropologists' label for the sum of the distinctive characteristics of a people's way of life."[28] When missionaries translate the language of a previously unreached people group, they must do it within the culture of that group. Language finds its meaning in terms of the culture.

In writings from the past, and in the present, there is much talk about the church being relevant. In the process, this has been described as being conformed to the world. The idea has been promoted that the church must be part of the world. Yet I maintain that the church must be in the world but not of it. Jesus addresses this issue:

> *"I have given them Your word; and the world has hated them*
> *because they are not of the world, just as I am not of the world.*
> *I do not pray that You should take them out of the world, but*
> *that You should keep them from the evil one. They are not of*
> *the world, just as I am not of the world."*
>
> —John 17:14–16

It must be understood that changing a culture requires time and focus. This is where focus on people in discipleship relationships becomes significant. Changes in culture will begin to take place one person at a time as they are given time and commitment. Even in small group discipleship ministries, the

---

28 Everett M. Rogers and Thomas M. Steinfatt, *Intercultural Communication*, Waveland Press, Prospect Heights Ill, 1999, p.266

change will take place one person at a time. This change will not happen through church growth conferences or seminars but through one-on-one ministry to each other. For conferences to bring that change would require each attendee accepting and applying the challenges presented. What conferences may do is affirm the culture of society or reflect the culture of the present. The present church culture should not be affirmed; an alternative must be offered.

Let me give examples of how church culture operates. If I ask, "How is your church doing?" I invariably get a response in numbers of people attending. But if this was what I wanted to know, I would have asked, "How many people are attending your church?" In a discipleship culture, numbers will not be an issue. A different question ought to be asked. Our thinking needs to be shifted to consider how people are doing in regard to growth and service.

Let me point out a caution about the power of manipulation of numbers. A report of an analysis of ministry in Northern Canada showed that the number of converts in a community amounted to more than the population of the community. The evangelists who gave those numbers went into the community a few times a year, and each time counted those who responded to their teaching as being new converts.

In another case, an analytical work was done on missionary activity in Haiti. The information for the study was taken from missionary prayer letters and reports from mission boards. After analyzing the numbers found in the literature over a period of some years, the analyst concluded that the entire population of Haiti was being saved every three years![29]

A 2015 conference of the Fellowship of Evangelical Baptist Churches of Canada was told by a plenary speaker that there were twenty things to watch for in churches in the future, one being an increased preference for smaller worship gatherings. This observation gives me hope because it speaks to a lessening of dependence on numbers. That will hopefully turn into a commitment to one-on-one or small group ministry which will include accountability.

I have heard people say of the Western church that "the Titanic has hit the iceberg, but the music is still playing." It appears the focus of the present church is on functioning culturally but not biblically, which is why the church therefore may be sinking.

There have been attempts to change the culture of the church, but most of those efforts have further diminished the faithfulness of the church to Scripture. However, these attempts have unfortunately succeeded to a degree by building a new culture of accommodation. Author Michael Horton has said, "We have created an environment of perpetual novelty."[30] We live in a culture of addictions, socially and church-wise, always looking for the newest and best fad. In a prominent New Monasticism

---

29 Peter Greer and Chris Horst, *Mission Drift*, Bethany House Publishers, Bloomington, Minnesota, 2015, p.128

30 Michael Horton, *Ordinary.* Zondervan, Grand Rapids, Mich, 2014, p.25

community house was a sign on the wall stating: "Everyone wants a revolution. Nobody wants to do the dishes."

The only answer that can be suggested to this cultural dilemma is that the focus must be on one-on-one or small group intentional discipleship, where we begin to change the thinking of individuals, one person at a time.

There must be three qualities to this process.

First, discipleship must be *intentional*. There must be a purpose to what is done relationally. More than being just a friend is required, although that will be included in a true discipling relationship. Application of the Word of God according to 2 Timothy 3:16–17 is essential:

> *All Scripture is given by inspiration of God, and is profitable for doctrine, for reproof, for correction, for instruction in righteousness, that the man of God may be complete, thoroughly equipped for every good work.*

I endeavour to get men to commit these verses to memory but find that there is often a very strong resistance against that discipline. Discipleship must have a goal which will dictate the type of material that is taught and discussed. I personally favour teaching the Scriptures rather that studying a book about the Scriptures.

Second, discipleship must be *accountable*. This is without doubt the most effective way to help a disciple to appropriate truth. Some will appropriate truth in a larger setting, such as a worship service, Sunday school, or perhaps even television, radio, or online ministry. This appropriation will require a highly motivated person, one who is adept at making application of truth without the help of another person. Many people in church do not fit that category. Therefore, accountability must be employed to bring about effective application. In school a student takes an exam to determine if he or she is retaining the information conveyed. That is not the purpose of discipleship. In discipleship, the gaining of information is not the final goal. The goal is an application of truth showing itself in the disciple learning to follow Christ in the everyday activities of life. Accountability can strain the discipleship relationship when the disciple has a difficult time putting into practice what he or she is learning.

Third, discipleship must be *measurable*. Growth must be evident in a believer's actions and attitude. If this is not happening, discipleship is not taking place.

I once met a lady from Michigan who had travelled to a small Ontario town to attend a wedding. She brought with her a twenty-one-year-old son, who was basically in a vegetative state. He had grown into adulthood physically, but not emotionally or functionally. I admired the mother's commitment to her son. It was evident that he had not developed as a fully functional human being, that the social and functional aspects of the young man had not developed. So it is that many people who profess faith in Christ are not seen to be developing spiritually. The discipler must encourage the disciple to talk about his or her spiritual growth, in order to show evidence of progress.

A church culture needs to be based on Scriptural demands, such as Matthew 28:18–20, Hebrews 10:24, and Luke 9:23. This speaks to a nurturing quality in the church. This quality of genuinely caring for each other must be based on a culture of truth. We are living in a post-truth era. We need to battle that destructive philosophy.

When people in church are offended by the teaching of truth, churches will too often seek to mollify the offended, rather than to affirm truth. Such an approach can only lead to compromise.

Will discipleship produce bigger churches? No, but it may produce more churches as individuals get involved in nurturing other believers. Churches will become smaller, so that a greater number of people can be involved in direct discipleship ministry. Churches need to be smaller so more people can serve, not bigger so more can attend and be entertained.

David Platt tells of visiting an impoverished church in Cuba that had planted sixty-five churches. He visited one of those sixty-five, of which one had planted another twenty-five more churches.[31] I doubt the church in Cuba has better resources or programs. The smaller churches will be where people can productively engage.

One objection heard from those who are not engaged in discipleship is that they cannot find the time. I bought into this

---

31 David Platt, *Radical,* Multnomah, Colorado Springs, Colorado, 2010, p.104

mindset to a degree during my years of ministry, but I look back with regret on the missed opportunities for more meaningful ministry to individuals. Everyone has exactly the same amount of time. It is not a matter of finding time, but of making time. It is a matter of choices based on priorities.

Jesus wandered through the streets and byways of Israel looking for a few people who would follow Him. He was initiating revolution, but His revolution would not revolve around the masses and multitudes. Instead it would revolve around a few men and women.[32]

---

32 David Platt, *Radical,* Multnomah, Colorado Springs, Colorado, 2010, p.88

Chapter Seven

DISCIPLESHIP IS A CALL TO ACTION

JESUS'S OWN WORDS ATTEST TO THIS: "*THEN HE SAID TO THEM ALL, 'If any one desires to come after Me, let him deny himself, and take up his cross daily, and follow Me.'*" (Luke 9:23). Then in Mark 10:21, we read:

> *Then Jesus, looking at him, loved him, and said to him, "One thing you lack: Go your way, sell whatever you have and give to the poor, and you will have treasure in heaven; and come, take up the cross, and follow Me."*
>
> —Mark 10:21

When spirituality is viewed as a static condition, the way to spiritual wholeness is seen as the acquisition of information and techniques that enable us to gain possession of the desired state of spirituality.[33] Thus our endless quest for techniques, methods, programs. I have visited churches demonstrating this

---

33 M. Robert Mulholland Jr., *Invitation to a Journey,* InterVarsity Press, Prospect Heights, Ill. 1993 p.12

restless quest for programs and methods. A church starts exciting programs, but workers are lacking to run those programs. That leads to people filling roles for which they are simply not equipped. Burnout is too often the end result of this way of "doing church." I have been in churches where the announcements on Sunday morning can be twenty minutes in length. Excess time spent on announcements is an indication of a church that is overly program-oriented.

Someone might think, "I am a Child of God, I am secure, all is fine." Another person says, "The goal has been accomplished. I have arrived." But this does not harmonize with Luke 9:23, where the call is to follow Jesus Christ. Jesus's call speaks of relationship and common purpose. "Follow me" is an expression of forward motion, not a static condition in which we simply exist. The word *if* is not a statement of expectation; it is rather an invitation, in which Christ leaves it up to the individual to make a decisive choice to follow Him. It is an invitation to a journey which will have ongoing obligations. To "*deny himself and take up his cross daily*" (Luke 9:23) requires constant forward motion. This is not a call to salvation, but to a commitment to *following* Jesus Christ. It is an invitation to a life-changing relationship. This is where discipleship enters in to help others to see the need for an ongoing and growing relationship with Christ.

An invitation to a discipleship class is not sufficient. Discipleship requires a relationship in order to be effective. Some might see a discipleship class as just another program, or as a means to do one's duty before God. Any program that takes the personal element out of discipleship will likely not be profitable.

I wrote earlier about the need for intentionality in discipleship. Merely gathering a group for Bible study will generally miss the mark. I am not saying we should not have group Bible studies, but we need to be more selective and intentional about the discipleship process. That is the surest way to minister to the needs of the individual. Our spiritual state is an ongoing journey. We must be intentional about helping others move forward on the path to greater spirituality.

Author Jim Cantelon gave a fine definition of discipleship on a television program. He said, "Discipleship is the discipline of following Jesus." That challenging word "discipline" must be fully engaged in the process of making disciples.

There are basic biblical teachings that we must come to understand and follow. These teachings must be taught and encouraged. People must be encouraged and challenged to exercise discipline in the process of learning and obeying. In a larger setting one cannot effectively address issues that people are dealing with on any given day. Addressing the particular issue a person is facing will happen best in a discipleship relationship. I see that as a nurturing process. I will address this concept in a later chapter. For now I will illustrate what I mean with a nurturing process.

At the time of writing, I have a very small backyard at my home. After a very hard and hot summer, I am not proud of it despite the time and effort my wife and I have put into it. The difference between attractive and unattractive yards is generally the amount of time and work that goes into them, but this is not a guarantee that the result will be great. It is true, though, that if no time and effort are put in, the results can hardly be good.

I try to take time to nurture the lawn, and my wife keeps our flowerbeds in attractive condition.

It can be discouraging when expectations are not met in the garden or in discipleship after time and effort have been expended. Disciple-making is not an easy process. It is trying. It is messy. It is slow, tedious, and even painful at times. It is all these things because it is relational.[34]

God outlines a definite and specific purpose for discipleship in the last part of 2 Timothy 3:17 which tells us we are to be fully equipped for every good work. In a discipling and nurturing relationship, our goal is to bring another to a state of growth and equipping. Equipping means here that an individual has gained the knowledge to teach and lead others in their walk with Christ. There is an objective and a process to reach that objective. The Scriptures are meant to be used in doctrine, for reproving, for correction, and for ongoing instruction in the righteous way of life.

Three steps are given in Luke 9:23 which instructs the follower of Christ to "*deny himself, and take up his cross daily, and follow me.*" In a nurturing relationship, disciples are helped to follow this prescribed pattern: first to become oblivious to self in the process of following Christ. The call is to self-denial instead of self-indulgence. The Apostle Paul illustrates this concept in 1 Corinthians 15:31 where he says, "*I die daily.*"

---

34 David Platt, *Radical*, Multnomah Press, Colorado Springs, Colorado, 2010, p.93

To deny ourselves is to put the past behind us, whether it is good or bad. It might be the awfulness of abuse or neglect, or it might be the acquiring of higher education. Neither of these ought to determine who we are. We use what is profitable in our past but do not count on it for credit. Paul rejected all his credentials, counting them as dung (Philippians 3:4–8). To leave everything behind is to be fully content with Christ.

When Peter denied knowing Jesus, it was because of self-preservation, rather than self-denial. Denying oneself is an ongoing, daily requirement; for most people, this demands a relationship of accountability. I have had the privilege of having two very dear friends from my days at Millar Memorial Bible Institute (now called Millar College of the Bible). The relationships which developed there became lifelong friendships of accountability in which we gave each other permission to speak words of correction as well as of encouragement.

To take up one's cross is to bear up under whatever life sends our way from day to day. It means to accept with humility the challenges that come our way, and to seek to please God on a daily basis.

To *"follow Me"* is to fall in line with the divine mission and purpose, even though there may be challenges to that commitment. The question is: how do we stay focused on following Christ?

I think of a time when my family and I were walking down a dirt road in a village in Ecuador. We noticed two black lines across the road. The first line consisted of ants carrying leaves from the left side of the road to the right side. Just beyond the first line, more ants were crossing in a line to the left to procure more leaves. I was puzzled by what they did because the foliage on both sides of the road looked exactly the same. The ants had a built-in sense of purpose, very much like what we need to possess in order to maintain our focus on Christ. I watched with great interest as a car came along and drove over some of the ants. I was fascinated by their demonstration of commitment. At the juncture where the tires had killed ants, those still carrying their leaves moved in circles for about three turns and then moved back in line as if nothing had happened. It took only about a minute until the lines were flowing smoothly again.

This demonstrates what happens in life when challenges strike. Firm commitment to the divine purpose may cause us to circle a few times to get refocused when disruption occurs, but then we will again follow the path set before us. We do not allow the difficulties to move us off course. This brings to mind the idea in Proverbs 6:6 that we should learn from the ants. At this point the nurturing of each other becomes a necessary practice. It gives us the blessing of having someone work with us in our difficulties as we follow the footsteps of Christ.

As I have said before, it is important to note when following Christ that there are no options; instead there are commands to obey.[35] Are we looking to Jesus for advice, or are we looking

---

35 David Platt, *Radical,* Multnomah, Colorado Springs. Colorado, Colorado, 2012, p.121

to Him for total leadership? He desires full and unconditional commitment, and on the journey of following Him, we have the blessing of having others in the body of Christ to nurture us. This is not a journey we are asked to travel alone.

The study books on the shelves of bookstores appear to be written on the basis of "one size fits all." However, I do not believe this to be a useful sentiment. We need to come alongside others and teach them and demonstrate to them what it is to follow Christ individually. Church culture has made the walk with Christ very personal, rather than corporate. Our allegiance to Christ is personal, but growth and productivity is rooted in relationship and discipleship. On this point, John Wesley is quoted as saying, "There can be no personal holiness without social holiness." A hunger for a nurturing discipleship ministry in the church needs awakening. Unfortunately, as James C. Wilhoit writes, "Our culture, and sadly that of many churches, seeks to squeeze us into the mold of merely being nice and seeking a sensible consumer-oriented faith that meets our needs and avoids offending anyone else."[36] If we are going to enter into the practice of discipleship, we will need to turn away from that type of expectation, and move into a culture of deliberate discipleship.

---

36 James C. Wilhoit, *Spiritual Formation as if the Church Mattered,* Baker Publishing, Grand Rapids, Mich, 2008, p.33

If our walk with Christ is going to enliven and enrich the Body of Christ, it must positively affect others in the Body.[37]

Mark 10:17–22 tells of a man who would have been an excellent candidate for membership in today's Western church. He was religious, rich, intelligent, eager, and likely influential. We would likely do everything possible to rope him in but Jesus did not make promises to him. Instead, because He loved him (Mark 10:21), Jesus told the man to remove from his affections everything that kept him from following Christ. In this case his wealth was what he loved more than following Christ.

The question then is, "Is Jesus worth abandoning everything for?" The answer, of course, must be a resounding "Yes!" Jesus loves people enough to tell them the truth. Since that was His approach to the training of people, can we do less?

At this point, we sometimes make a mistake. We tend to see the call to discipleship as a call to do the unusual. But discipleship is not a call to a series of extraordinary events; it is a call to an ordinary Christian life. In terms of today's mediocre Christian living, a change to a discipleship culture might look radical but what we perceive as radical should be the ordinary life of commitment to discipleship. Instead of making a distinction between radical and ordinary, I would distinguish between ordinary and carnal (1 Corinthians 3). It should be unusual and even outrageous for the ordinary believer to pile up possessions.

---

37 M. Robert Mulholland Jr., *Invitation to a Journey,* InterVarsity Press, Prospect Heights, Ill, 1993, p.14

For the rich young man in the Mark story, the cost of discipleship was too high. But frankly, the cost of non-discipleship is vastly higher.

Chapter Eight

DISCIPLESHIP WITH RESULTS

LET ME INTRODUCE YOU TO A UNIQUE MAN. HE WAS UNIQUE BECAUSE he was the only man. He was unique because he was the first man.

> *Then the Lord God took the man and put him in the garden of Eden to tend and keep it. And the Lord God commanded the man, saying, "Of every tree of the garden you may freely eat; but of the tree of the knowledge of good and evil you shall not eat, for in the day that you eat of it you shall surely die."*
> —Genesis 2:15–17

The man received instructions from God. No one else was present so he knew God was addressing him. He is referred to as "*the man,*" because he was the only one. The woman came later, in verse 18; she did not hear the conversation between God and the man.

The question *Has God said…?* plants a seed of doubt, even today, and is a very effective strategy. In the garden, the devil reinterpreted what God had said. He moved God's commands from the spiritual to the physical-sensual. 1 Timothy 2:14 says Eve was deceived by the devil. What should the man, Adam, have done? He should have protected Eve with the knowledge he had, having received it directly from God. Genesis 3:2–3 indicates that she had been told of the instructions, but it did not come to her directly from God. The man who had the direct communication from God did not uphold the Word of God. John Eldridge says Adam "gave away the essence of his strength."[38] Instead of speaking up protectively, he tried to blame her: "*Then the man said, 'The woman whom you gave to be with me, she gave me of the tree, and I ate'*"(Genesis 3:12). Adam should have protected her by holding to the revealed Word of God. The essence of his strength should have been godly convictions (God had spoken) followed by bold action to protect the woman who faced deception.

That obligation and responsibility still stands today. 2 Timothy 2:2 tells us, "*And the things that you have heard from me among many witnesses, commit these to faithful men who will be able to teach others also.*" We are to pass on the baton. In Matthew 28:20, Jesus gives commands: go, make disciples, baptize, and teach them to observe God's commands. This principle of upholding the Word of God in protection is still true today. It is best expressed in discipleship of others.

As noted previously, in the process of discipling, consider the purpose of the Word of God. In 2 Timothy 3:16–17, the purpose of the Word is to bring believers to a place where they are useful and effective in God's service. They are to be equipped

---

38 John Eldridge, *Wild at Heart,* Thomas Nelson, Nashville, TN, 2001, p.143

for every good work. This is the nature of intentional discipleship, where men meet with men and women meet with women to teach and learn how to apply the Scriptures to their own lives, and to uphold biblical truth. In this process, what God has said is shared, and protection from deception is thus given to another.

Pastor Randy Visconti of Generation Church in Arizona said in a sermon that you can follow Christ for yourself, but you cannot follow Christ by yourself. The Body of Christ is interdependent. Some words used in the Bible to describe our interactions in discipleship include provoke, teach, and admonish. They convey the idea of community.

Mark Sayers has said, "I became focused on passing the baton to others, stepping out of the way so others could flourish."[39] Like Sayers, I want to pass the baton to others who are trained in the Word of God to help them become *"equipped for every good work"* (2 Timothy 3:17). This is the sense in which we need to take care of each other in nurturing relationships.

Fellowship can be an effective vehicle for discipleship, provided it is intentional. Although we can enjoy informal, spontaneous fellowship with no particular purpose other than unwinding and laughing, we need to give attention to fellowship for the purpose of spiritual ministry to each other.

Hebrews 10:24 uses fellowship as a vehicle for discipleship when it says, *"And let us consider one another in order to stir up love and good works."* To "consider" is to observe, to perceive. To "stir

---

39 Mark Sayers, *Christianity Today,* October 2014, pp 52-57

up" is to provoke or to bring to action. If these two attitudes have a meaningful presence in our lives, we can have an impact on others to bring them to a place of being equipped for service to God and to one another.

What is the result when discipleship is not practised? This is illustrated with a story I heard from a missionary in Indonesia. While visiting one of the islands, this missionary met a young man near a large church. He asked the man if he attended church. The man assured him he did, because it was one of the three laws. The missionary asked what the three laws were, and the man was surprised that the missionary would not know something so obvious. He explained that the three laws are: go to church, do not sleep with married women, and dress appropriately. The missionary asked why one needed to keep these laws, and the man explained that you keep the laws to get ready for the Great Coming Again. When quizzed about the Great Coming Again, the missionary was told it was the occasion when you died and went to heaven where you are judged for the way you have kept the three laws. Then you return to earth and you are born again.

This is classic syncretism (the blending of different religions into one), including beliefs in reincarnation and salvation by works. This heresy occurs when the Word of God is not taught, learned, and practised as God's absolute truth. Neglect of truth leads to error.

My Indonesian host and I drove to village churches on two Sunday mornings and observed people walking to church, dressed well and carrying Bibles. My host assured me it was all formality, where they obeyed on the outside, but actually lived as they pleased.

A statement by Dallas Willard is very appropriate and applicable here: "Your system is perfectly designed to produce the results you are getting."[40] This system was built on compliance, where Bible knowledge and the work of the Holy Spirit were not needed.

Jesus did not tell us to go into all the world and tell them to behave but to go and make disciples. In view of this, the church needs to ask itself, "What are we trying to accomplish? What methods are we going to use to get to the goal?" The best method will be to walk shoulder to shoulder with someone and show him or her how to walk the path of faith. In the process, we teach people how to read and study Scripture.

It has been my observation that when men are asked to read a passage for observation that they will take about two seconds and then wait for the teacher to give the right interpretation! Observation must become a vital part of the process of understanding and applying the truths of Scripture. One veteran preacher of old was known to read a text forty times before he would proceed with his study. This is a strong commitment to observation and would be an excellent investment of our time.

If we do not engage in such practices, we encourage a perpetual adolescence. James Montgomery is quoted as saying:

---

40 James C. Wilhoit, *Spiritual Formation as if the Church Mattered,* Baker Publishing, Grand Rapids, Mich, 2008, p.37

"Instead of the Biblical pattern of children growing toward maturity, churches were turning adults into children."[41] I think back fondly to my time in youth group in the 1950s, when we were challenged to exercise gifts and abilities based on learning of Scripture. We were encouraged toward maturity. Many youth groups today seem to encourage members to stay in dependent adolescence.

In discipleship, we teach learners, so to speak, to chew their spiritual food properly in order to digest Scripture well. I recall as a child seeing my mother pre-chew food for my younger siblings, so they would be able to swallow it, and thus benefit from it.

Discipling is concerned about what people will become. We are too often guilty of assigning value to people based on what they do.[42] We ought to be concerned about character first, actions second. 1 John 1:9 says God will *"cleanse us from all unrighteousness."* That is character development until, as Galatians 4:19 says, *"Christ is formed in you."*[43] It is not simply a matter of imitating Him as best we can, but Christ being formed in us. That requires a nurturing community, a nurturing relationship.

In 2 Timothy 2:22, Paul instructs Timothy to pursue righteousness, faith, love, peace. But there is a second part of that instruction in that verse: Paul adds *"with those who call on the Lord*

---

41 Michael Horton, *Ordinary,* Zondervan, Grand Rapids, Mich., 2014, p.47

42 M. Robert Mulholland Jr., *Invitation to a Journey,* InterVarsity Press, Prospect Heights, Ill. 1993, p.29

43 Ibid, p.321

out of a pure heart." We are to develop these qualities with others who love the Lord, to do this in community.

This requires two things. We need to have passion for the spiritual health of men, women and children, pouring our life and experience into the lives of others. We also need to cultivate diligence and determination in the study and teaching of the Word of God. The word "excellence" comes to mind here. Change the emphasis from teaching to teaching *and* learning. A former student of Dr. Howard Hendricks (a professor at Dallas Theological Seminary) said Dr. Hendricks held the view that if his student failed, he had failed. We need to take responsibility for the learning our students-disciples achieve. It has been my experience in some situations the teaching has been good, but the learning has been a failure. This is where the one-on-one discipling relationship will accomplish much more. In intentional discipleship, we focus on the learning that takes place as well as the teaching. This means that discipleship occurs at the speed of the disciple.

Chapter Nine

DISCIPLESHIP IN A NURTURING CONTEXT

THERE IS A FINE BALANCE IN NATURE. ECOSYSTEMS ARE WEBS OF interdependent life. Upset the balance and there is loss. For example, the shortage of bees and butterflies in recent years is a concern because it upsets the ecological balance; pollination drops drastically without sufficient numbers of these insects.

In church, balance is disrupted because programs and entertainment have become disproportional. There is more interest in bringing people in for programs than nurturing those already sought out. I referred earlier to a question invariably asked when pastors gather for fellowship: "How is your church doing?" The answer generally comes back in terms of numbers in attendance, which then leads to budget figures. This answer says volumes about the culture of the church.

If I met a dairy farmer and asked him, "How is your farm doing?" I'm not asking how many cows he has on the farm. I don't care how many sick, feeble, unproductive cows he has on the farm. I want to know how much milk they are producing. That is the bottom line in terms of having milk cows on the farm.

A question has been asked regarding church: Are we feeding the sheep, or entertaining the goats? If our purpose is entertaining, numbers will matter. If our purpose is discipling, numbers will not be the focus. The practice of discipleship has been seriously minimized. The church is not only an institution with a systematic theology; it is an organism with a form of life. A consumerist approach says the church should jealously guard what it has and thinks is valuable. The obligation seems to be to build a fence around ourselves to keep us in. However, in Matthew 16:18 Jesus says of the church, *"...the gates of hell shall not prevail against it."* Gates are an instrument of protection, so the church is to be on the attack against the forces of evil. There is an urgency to prepare ourselves and others for the battle. This is most effectively done by discipling the young people in a church. We seem to worry more about other churches stealing our people than about the world stealing them. The fact is that the world steals far more of our youth than do other churches. Surveys have indicated that only about ten percent of church youth who attend university continue to attend church services. The cause is the lack of the nurturing quality of discipleship.

It troubles me that some young men in one church I pastored walked away from any connection with the church. I often wonder what I could have done differently to prevent their exit. I believe I could have trained more people to disciple these young men to be well grounded in the Scriptures.

When young people start to build a home, some come back to the church for the sake of their children. When they do come back, they need training and nurturing. Will the church have a discipleship mentality so these young families can be ministered to effectively? A commitment needs to be in place to disciple them.

There are so many references in Scripture to gardening,[44] and the nurturing that goes with gardening. Michael Horton drew my attention to this emphasis.[45] A productive garden is the result of nurturing. It is noteworthy that when God created man and woman, He placed them in a garden. Adam's first job description, so to speak, was the maintenance of the garden. Then as punishment for disobedience he and Eve were banished from the garden. After the Fall, pleasure was removed from gardening and was replaced by weeds and sweat.

The garden was a significant part of my growing-up years. To feed the sixteen siblings in our family required a huge garden, and Mother kept it well. At that time sugar beets were very popular as a cash crop and Dad would hire us out to farmers to weed their fields. We would hoe out the excessive beet plants to about twenty centimetres apart so there would be room for them to grow to their intended size. Any plants closer together than this were removed. Then we would remove all the weeds, so that the nourishment of the field would be allowed to sustain the beets which were left. The fields were thus carefully nurtured.

I also learned many lessons from what the Bible says about gardening. Psalm 1:3 indicates there is a process of planting,

---

44 Psalm 1:3-4, Isaiah 5:2-6, Jeremiah 2:21, 12:10, Hosea 14:4-8, Matthew 3:10, 13:1-9, 24-32, Luke 16:6-9, John 15:1-5, 1 Corinthians 3:5-9

45 Michael Horton, *Ordinary,* Zondervan, Grand Rapids, Mich. 2014, p.169

watering, and waiting. Isaiah 5:1–6 speaks to the gardening process to illustrate God's work, and the disappointment of not seeing proper development. In 1 Corinthians, the Apostle Paul using the gardening analogy of planting, watering, and waiting for growth.

God declares His love for the nurturing process by the garden of Eden, and by the passion He has given parents for nurturing their children. So the community of believers must of necessity be a place of nurturing.

I have also observed what happens when we don't focus on nurturing. In my years of pastoring I have noticed a very observable fact: when nurturing is not common, conflict will be. As attention turns inward it will produce conflict.

I keep my lawn, which I referred to earlier, small as it is, in good shape by tending it carefully rather than merely cutting the grass. I fertilize it four times a year to keep the grass thick and healthy. The care I give the lawn goes a long way toward guarding against the intrusion of weeds.

There are two noteworthy lessons we can take from the process of nurturing plants and apply to nurturing disciples: it is slow, and it is a lot of work.[46] Nurturing affects everyone in church. Large numbers of people in pastoral work take medical leave due to stress. That happens because there is not enough accountable nurturing taking place. We need to surround ourselves with people who will nurture our souls. My wife has over the

---

46 Michael Horton, *Ordinary,* Zondervan, Grand Rapids, Mich, 2014, p.173

years been a wonderful sounding board, who has helped alleviate a lot of stress in my life.

A note about burnout might be profitable here. An elderly couple, married sixty-five years, wrote a series of life lessons for their children and grandchildren. One of these was the following:

> If you find that Christianity exhausts you, draining you of your energy, then you are practicing religion rather than enjoying a relationship with Jesus Christ. Your walk with the Lord will not make you weary; it will invigorate you, restore your strength, and energize your life.[47]

This advice is supported by Matthew 11:28–29.

One reason why discipleship has lost its edge is that the expectations are unclear, or even absent. The one who is being discipled should identify for the discipler the needs he or she wishes to address. Likewise, the discipler should tell the disciple what strengths he or she will bring to the relationship. This is where the culture of the church must change to become a nurturing fellowship.

I am accountable to God, not to people, therefore I must maintain that kind of relationship with Christ so I can stand for truth and impart it to others. That is why I am not concerned about numbers and budget. I am concerned about people being

---

47 David Mccasland, *Daily Bread*, Grand Rapids, MIch. June 14, 2017

nurtured so they can lead others to maturity, as seen in 1Timo-thy 2:2. I do not want to offend with my own actions and reactions, but if they are offended by the truth, that is between them and God.

We must return to the practice of giving one another permission to hold each other accountable, allowing nurturing to actually take place, taking spiritual responsibility for each other, according to Hebrews 10:24, which says, *"And let us consider one another in order to stir up love and good works"* and Colossians 3:16:

> *Let the word of Christ dwell in you richly in all wisdom, teaching and admonishing one another in psalms and hymns and spiritual songs, singing with grace in your hearts to the Lord.*

Lewis Smedes tells of seeing his good friend Carl Bultuis after hearing that Bultuis had terminal cancer. Lewis spent a week with his friend. During that time Bultuis called Lewis's attention to some flaws he had noticed in Lewis. After pointing them out, he said he hoped Lewis would work to correct them. Lewis concluded that they should have been more open and more emotionally sensitive toward each other all along.[48] In the process of discipleship we need to build a relationship of trust that will allow us to be increasingly open with each other in accountability.

---

48 Lewis Smedes, *Shame and Grace,* Zondervan, Grand Rapids, Mich. 1993, p.126

Our commitment to personal growth in Christ should remove the element of taking offense when corrected.

The emphasis on nurturing is unmistakable in John 5:5–9:

Now a certain man was there who had an infirmity thirty-eight years. When Jesus saw him lying there, and knew that he already had been in that condition *a long time, He said to him, "Do you want to be made well?" The sick man answered Him, "Sir, I have no man to put me into the pool when the water is stirred up; but while I am coming, another steps down before me." Jesus said to him, "Rise, take up your bed and walk." And immediately the man was made well, took up his bed, and walked.*

The crippled man had been in his condition for thirty-eight years, and had been in the proximity of the healing waters of the pool of Bethesda for a long time. Jesus asked him if he wanted to be well. We might wonder why he had not gotten into the water when it had been stirred up before. The man's answer is heart-wrenching. "*I have no man to put me into the pool.*" What was the man's greatest need? Some kind of revival service, or some kind of incantation? No, he needed someone to stand with him in his need, a friend and discipler. There are so many who are wandering aimlessly, even though they may have been attending church faithfully. They need someone to meet them in their greatest need, who can give them direction in their spiritual development.

I say there is a need for nurturing here, because the man needed someone to help with something he could not do for himself. He undoubtedly had people around him, since there was always someone who got to the pool first, but there was no one who is able to help him in his need. There is a lesson to be learned here that there are people in need of someone else, thus the emphasis on nurturing.

A question can be posed in the context of trying to be there for someone in their time of need: is the ministry we are engaged in sustainable? Sustaining a program-oriented church ministry will lead to stress and burnout. Workers get tired and discouraged with what is needed to keep programs running. Another means of doing the job needs to be implemented. Relational ministry is a sustainable approach. It allows for a fellowship for both parties that will encourage continuation of the relationship. This ministry also has the capacity to influence generations, as seen in 2 Timothy 2:2: There is a four-generation exercise expressed in the passage: Paul disciples the second generation, Timothy, who in turn teaches a third generation, who teaches a fourth. One generation alone will never complete this task. This shows the sustainable nature of discipleship when it is practiced intentionally.

The difficult part in church ministry will be letting go of that which the church culture has presumed to be good and needful. But really only preaching Christ and discipleship are essential. When efforts to make these two goals effective take place, a good balance will be achieved. The process of discipleship will go against the grain of our instant-gratification culture and acquisitive society. Author James C. Wilhoit says, "Our culture and, sadly, many churches, seek to squeeze us into the mold of merely being nice and seeking a sensible consumer-oriented faith that meets our needs and avoids offending anyone else."[49] We are consumers of Christian services and programs which can replace obedience to Christ.

Wilhoit says that "Spirituality, for many, has become merely another dimension of Christian consumerism."[50] Church culture has adopted a *me first* mentality, which is very much opposed to Philippians 2:3: "*Let nothing be done through selfish ambition or conceit, but in lowliness of mind let each esteem others better than himself.*" It is the relational side of ministry that will persevere and be productive. The joy and fulfillment found in watching the garden grow as well as seeing fruit from one season to another will be ours in a nurturing and discipling relationship.

A gentleman I was discipling told me he thought about something I had said regarding a Scripture passage, recognized its value for his need of the moment, and talked to the Lord about it. He is to be commended for taking it to the Lord rather than talking to his me. That growth pattern is what ought to be the desired goal of our ministry to others. Encourage and challenge the disciple to seek the Lord; desire to see people take

---

49 James C. Wlihoit, *Spiritual Formation as if the Church Mattered*, Baker Publishing, Grand Rapids, Mich, 2008, p.33

50 Ibid, p.52

responsibility for their walk with Christ. That is progress in the growing the garden of the soul.

The garden does not grow in some sensational outburst; it does so in the growth pattern of nature. What makes it such a thing of beauty is the normative nature of growth.

We tend to view what we see in the church as normal, and expect anyone radical, few as they may be, to take up what the Scriptures demand. It appears we have accepted the idea there are committed Christians (radical) and fleshly, materialistic Christians who see themselves as normal Christians. But according to 1 Corinthians 3:1–3, the committed Christians are the normal Christians, while the fleshly and materialistic Christians are not. Paul writes,

> *And I, brethren, could not speak to you as to spiritual people but as to carnal, as to babes in Christ. I fed you with milk and not with solid food; for until now you were not able to receive it, and even now you are still not able; for you are still carnal. For where there are envy, strife, and divisions among you, are you not carnal and behaving like mere men?*

Our task is to disciple others to move on from the fleshly and materialistic condition to victory, as they come to know and love the Lord. Wilhoit says,

> The Church of Jesus Christ is present when people gather together in the power of the Risen Christ, as demonstrated in the nurturing of each other. To

avoid spiritual bankruptcy and decay we must nurture each other.[51]

The nature of this nurturing ministry is alluded to in Matthew 23:37:

O Jerusalem, Jerusalem, the one who kills the prophets and stones those who are sent to her! How often I wanted to gather your children together, as a hen gathers her chicks under her wings, but you were not willing!

and Isaiah 66:13: *"As one whom his mother comforts, so I will comfort you; and you shall be comforted in Jerusalem."*

---

51 James C. Wilhoit, *Spiritual Formation as if the Church Mattered,* Baker Publishing, Grand Rapids, Mich. 2008, p.34

Chapter Ten

DISCIPLESHIP AND ITS VALUE

THE VALUE OF DISCIPLESHIP IS SEEN IN THE APOSTLE PAUL'S LETTER TO Timothy (2 Timothy 3:16-17) which describes how the disciple will become mature and an effective servant. This chapter will look at four elements of value that are produced in a discipling and nurturing relationship.

Discipleship provides focus.

In a discipleship ministry, the seed is not scattered at random. We will be able to have selected hearers and followers. The seeding process will be geared to an individual, or a small group. It will meet the individual's needs. This is what makes the growth measurable; the results are visible as one interacts with the disciples. The chances of growth are much greater than when spreading the seed at random. Pastoral testimony indicates we can be too busy with expectations of public services to be able to give adequate time to individual ministry. Perhaps less public teaching and preaching, and more emphasis on discipleship will produce a better product. This leads to the next quality of importance.

Discipleship provides accountability and assessment.

Accountability will not always be popular. In fact, it may seldom be welcomed. That raises the question of whether we want to be popular or effective. Our society goes out of its way to honour celebrities and sports stars, so the pull of popularity is often the strongest. The culture of society has become the culture of the church, so we have the religious superstars. Despite this unfortunate state of affairs, to the credit of the church, there has recently been a significant change in the dynamics of Sunday church meetings. It used to be expected that the pastor would meet the people at the front door, where things were often said that were not meant. Today we see pastors mingling much more so there is more genuine spiritual fellowship.

There will be those who will disappoint us in the process of accountability. There is a price to pay for the disciple, as seen in Luke 9:23, where the disciple is urged to "*deny himself.*" The same principle is seen in Mark 10:17–22 where the expectation is that the man will not allow his wealth to be his top priority. Unfortunately it appears that he was not willing to pay that price.

Discipleship gives meaning to goal-setting.

Disciple-making must be measurable. It has been a common thought among pastors that their job is to teach the Word and to allow the Holy Spirit to make the appropriate application. That is a wonderful concept and is true in certain situations. I will not deny that principle, but neither will I use it as an excuse. It seems that, for the church, discipleship is not a priority. We may dabble in it by claiming that discipleship should be happening, but too often we substitute programs for relationship. The command of Matthew 28:18–20 is to make disciples and teach them to observe what we have been commanded. This means to encourage them to practise the teaching of Scripture, as is also stated as far back as Joshua 1:8. The best way to know if people are observing, and acting on what Jesus taught, is by being in a position to observe and discuss their application of the truth.

We can learn from Peter (Acts 10) and from Philip (Acts 8) that God uses people to convey truth. The church is looking for methods; God is looking for people. Matthew 10 finds Jesus sending the Twelve out as sheep among wolves. It is unlikely that their work was done by formal meetings, but by contact with individuals. To be *"wise as serpents and harmless as doves"* (Matthew 10:16) would surely be in the context of individual contacts and relationships. It is through the training of people for missionary service by organizations like Ethnos Canada, (formerly New Tribes Mission of Canada) that we see the incredible value of relationships. In the learning of language and culture (over years, not weeks), missionaries must of necessity give much attention to relationships. Because of this process, when the gospel is taught, and people respond to the gospel, the opportunities for discipleship are ready and productive.

The life of Moses illustrates the value of time invested. In Exodus 3:6, Moses is at first afraid to see the Lord God. But later, in Exodus 33:18 he is anxious to see the Lord. A whole lot of growth has taken place while he was separated from the crowds. His relationships would have been one-on-one, or small groups. This is where the culture of the church fails us. We are required to work to make a difference and change things, knowing the Lord is the key. As Psalm 46:10 teaches us, change and growth take place more effectively in our quietness before God, and in the accountability of relationships.

Discipleship will keep us normal.

There is a tendency in the church to focus on the next big fad, or on celebrities or sports stars. Youth are often encouraged to embrace this culture, with churches trying to win them over by excitement. In such a setting, which glorifies stardom in its worldly sense, a plain man or woman devoted to spreading the teachings of Christ may seem uninspiring, a model few will wish to follow.

But youth need teaching that following Christ in a very practical and obedient fashion is the normal Christian life. Instead of inviting a celebrity to a youth meeting, why don't we invite the couple who have been married for forty or fifty years and let them share how they have remained true to their commitment to each other? This interaction would benefit those not yet married, or newly married, to hear how to work through the rough spots and make marriage work in the biblical pattern. Attention must be given to promoting the practical instead of the sensational, reality instead of the excitement of outward exuberance. One method may be exciting, but the other is productive.

Discipleship emphasizes the ordinary.[52] Unfortunately, there is a tendency to describe ministries in ways beyond our reach. We are passionate about superlatives, including advocating for the Christian life as if it were meant only for spiritual

---

52 Michael Horton, *Ordinary,* Zondervan, Grand Rapids, Mich. 2014, p.8

heroes while the rest of us stand on the sidelines cheering on the few. The emphasis is on the radical, the unusual. The result is a sense of restlessness as we seek the next big thing. We need to become restless with our restlessness. The pursuit of the radical, the new, will leave us always looking, never being content.

Discipled people need to become fully normal in the life of following Christ. It will take two or three generations to get to a place where obedience to Christ moves from radical to normal.

The Apostle Paul appears to be imploring every Christian to strive for that kind of life. This proposed change will best come when we take personal interest in believers and disciple them to obedience. Right now, far too many are falling through the cracks. They do not see that the lives they are living are far from the expectations in Scripture.

Discipleship is the ministry with the best chance of bringing people to an understanding of what a follower of Christ will be like. Biblical discipleship will lead the disciple's lifestyle to become contrary to the present culture of society. Michael Horton has a very gentle way of addressing this concept. "Maybe if we discover the opportunities of the ordinary, a fondness for the familiar, and marvel again at the mundane, we will be radical after all."[53] We need men and women who will be willing to remain faithful living out the faith without looking for the sensational. There is no need to seek for shortcuts in the process.

---

53 Ibid, p.27

A missionary couple from Honduras arrived in Florida for furlough, and went shopping for groceries. She was used to cooking from scratch, so she was looking for plain unseasoned rice. Of the many kinds of rice on the shelves, she said she could not find any rice that was not pre-cooked or pre-seasoned. Similarly, we are very adept at using shortcuts in the process of church ministry. We focus on greater speed and less effort, the "bigger, better, more" of the American Dream. The church is encouraged to adapt to what people want, thus making them feel better about themselves. However, the better advice is to set a biblical course and persevere.

Leroy Eims tells of meeting a veteran missionary who attended to the usual missionary programs. In the same area, there was also a young missionary named Johnny who did mission work differently, spending the bulk of his time with a few young men. The veteran missionary tried to straighten Johnny out, but Johnny kept on with his plodding approach. The years passed and the veteran missionary who left the field for retirement sat in the Eims's living room and recounted his years of ministry. In retrospect he had little to show for his years of effort, admitting that he had left no disciples behind to carry on the work. He recounted Johnny's life and saw his ministry had led to one man being a university professor, who was being using mightily by God. Another was discipling a group of forty young men and women. Another of his disciples had a group of thirty-five young disciples around him of which three had gone to other countries as discipling missionaries. He said, "When I looked at Johnny's ministry it seemed so insignificant, but the results after the years are staggering."[54]

54 Leroy Eims, *The Lost Art of Disciple Making,* Zondervan/NavPress, Grand Rapids, Mich. 1978, p.23

Chapter Eleven

DISCIPLESHIP IN THE LOCAL CHURCH

IT HAS BEEN SAID THE CHURCH HAS MISSIONS BECAUSE IT DOES NOT have worship. It may well be that programs have replaced worship of God. A commercialized human-centred church does not lead people in a genuine worship of the Triune God. The fact that the church has become commercialized is evident by the fact that in Western culture it has become budget-driven. An addiction to programs is the centre of budget focus, rather than training people in discipleship and turning them loose to nurture each other. In the budget system there is a fine line between success and failure because we are so seriously affected in budget by any adversity which can seriously affect donations. If there is a snowstorm that closes a church, the budget may be out of balance for the whole year.

Budgets tend to tie the hands of leadership because they do not allow spending as needed. I would suggest developing a church budget that allows for spending in the moment rather than being tied to predetermined amounts. In many cases the ministry of a church is determined by adherence to a budget rather than the needs of people to be discipled and trained.

These budget issues have the potential of causing frustration and mistrust, and lead people to change churches or to abandon church attendance altogether.

The other issue needing to be addressed is a misdirected sense of worship. One needs only to sit through a few church services to realize that much of worship is focused on the performers on the platform. Terms such as "worship wars" show us the extent to which we have operated in the flesh as we have pursued "worship" in a most carnal fashion. I don't say this to discourage the reader, but to point out that there is something amiss in the functioning of the church so that we can find our way back to what Jesus intended when He made the pronouncement, "*I will build my church*" (Matthew 16:18).

I would enjoy seeing and experiencing a church assembly sharing the joy of the growth of their disciples. That would leave very little room for conflict. It appears too many people do not possess an understanding of how to apply the teaching and principles of Scripture to their lives and relationships in order to function as contributing members of a local church body. This is where intentional discipleship can be highly effective. The solution to this dilemma begins with an exciting understanding of the passage we call the Great Commission (Matthew 28:18-20), in which Jesus says we are to go, make disciples, baptize, and teach. Based on the experience of Jesus and the Apostle Paul we must recognize that the ongoing teaching involves application and accountability. This speaks of relationships, not programs.

Jesus said in Matthew 7:21–23 that there will be people who try to impress Him with the good things they have done. They have done these good things without a godly and honourable reason. Doing without being does not please the Lord, as we saw in the Sin Continuum earlier: God cares first about our being. One church I attended appears to be very successful with three Sunday morning services. However, there is a problem: there is great difficulty finding volunteers to run the programs they feel are required to maintain their success. I would say that if qualified workers to run the program are lacking, end the program. What they see as success I see as dismal failure. They are placing huge stress on the workers, sometimes to the point of burnout. This also emphasizes the need for discipleship and training.

Jesus's response to the people who did good things in Matthew 7 was to tell them to depart from Him, because He never knew them. This speaks loudly of Jesus's emphasis on relationships instead of programs. As Robert Mulholland so aptly describes it, "They were so busy in the world for God that they failed to be in God for the world."[55] We can be guilty of hiding behind a wall of activity, taking our identity or value from that activity. Our identity must come from our relationship with Christ. I am first a Child of God, then a pastor or any other occupation. Perhaps the praise received due to our busyness becomes our idol. We need to do with our busyness what the Apostle Paul did with his credentials: counted them loss for Christ, seeing them as rubbish (Philippians 3:8–10). Perhaps a good rebuke

---

55 M. Robert Mulholland Jr., *The Deeper Journey,* InterVarsity Press, Prospect Heights, Ill. 2006, p.47

to the sentiment of activity would be found in Psalm 46:10: "*Be still, and know that I am God.*" Paradoxically, the greatest threat to devotion to Christ is activity for Christ.

It has been suggested that discipleship disregards evangelism. I have been blessed to be able to disciple people *to* Christ as well as *in* Christ. Without evangelism there is no need or purpose for discipleship. Without discipleship, evangelism will be very limited. The most effective evangelism comes from relationship, due to the built-in follow-up dictated by the relationship. We are to be in the world for the spiritual welfare of people we befriend.

A walk with Christ may be seen as of secondary importance to the attaining of the American Dream. A culture focused on self can only worship self.

Each individual church is subject to a certain culture that dictates how the church views itself as wll as the lost condition of humanity. A look at the culture of the church in Germany in the time of Dietrich Bonhoeffer will be profitable. This was a time when the church needed to experience all the nurturing the church community had to offer. However, Bonhoeffer encountered self-serving accommodation to evil and an open endorsement of the Hitler regime by the church. Bonhoeffer was hated by the German regime because he was outspoken against Hitler's direction for the nation. Thus he was executed in the last days of the war in anticipation of the end of hostilities. The church culture of the time was one of fear and accommodation. A dear friend of mine was a teenager during that time and he came to hate all churches and ministers. He reacted bitterly toward the culture of accommodation the church had established. A Christian lady developed a vibrant relationship with the gentleman and eventually he did come around to respecting the church and its ministers, through her caring and instruction in the things of God.

If we are all about "bigger and better," discipleship does not fit in because it does not produce "bigger and better." Discipleship builds quality and perseverance. The local church must begin to establish the nurturing culture needed to develop passionate followers of Christ, and not seeking the benefits of pleasure and secularism.

To produce true maturity in believers, all the members of the local church must become committed to the nurturing of one another.

Chapter Twelve

DISCIPLESHIP IN PRACTICE

My intention in writing this book has been to educate and equip followers of Christ for the practice of discipleship in the setting of the modern church. Some suggestions may be helpful in terms of beginning the practice of discipleship.

Discipleship can be one of the most rewarding aspects of the Christian experience and needs to be practised with conviction and passion. The advice given here is not to be construed as a program to follow. It must be evaluated on an individual basis, according to the strengths and needs of both individuals involved in the relationship.

One needs to base a disciple-making relationship on the needs, strengths, goals, and personality of the disciple. One should not impose an expectation on the disciple that does not speak to the direct needs of that individual. Therefore a relationship must be established in order to determine those issues. It must be a relationship that is open on both sides, and is established on the basis of understanding of each other.

Biblical discipleship must be based on the nature and authority of Scripture. The disciple must be led to an understanding that the follower of Christ must order his or her life by the teachings of Scripture, and by the example of others who have walked with Christ. Teaching the disciple how to study Scripture in a way that cultivates an understanding of the entirety of God's Word will be one of the most urgent exercises. One of the least desired but most useful exercises in getting to know the Bible is by memorization. If we are going to meditate on the Scriptures day and night (Joshua 1:8), memorization makes it accessible at any time. A discipler must use the Scriptures in making application of whatever life brings in the disciple's path.

God commands us to pray, and we see the importance of prayer in Jesus's life. A disciple needs to understand that prayer is an exercise of communing with God. If we are to pray without ceasing (1 Thessalonians 5:17) we need to see prayer as relating to all aspects of life.

It is very important for the disciple to realize that the view we have of the greatness of God will impact the way we live life as a follower of Christ. He or she needs to be taught that the greatness, glory and majesty of the Trinity are expressed in praise throughout Scripture. It is a beneficial exercise to walk through the Old Testament to see illustrations of the greatness of God, in terms of who He is and what He does.

The process of discipleship involves determining weaknesses in the life of the disciple, in order to assist in finding solutions to these needy issues. The discipler will also need to determine the strengths of the disciple in order to equip him or her for service to the Lord (1 Timothy 3:16–17). Discipleship will not merely impart greater knowledge of Scripture but will assist the disciple in becoming a spiritual blessing to both the Christian and secular communities, through obedience to Scripture.

A few elements of a discipling relationship will produce understanding and commitment in the life of the disciple. The follower of Christ will develop other elements that come from his or her passion for the church, and from the relationship on which it will be based. This commitment will depend on a nurturing relationship that seeks to produce disciples who will in turn disciple others. This process can lead to exponential growth in the church of Jesus Christ over a few generations.

CONCLUSION

In the 1970s Christians endeavoured to copy a revival program from one part of Canada to another. The result would have been hilarious if it had not been so sad. The mentality seemed to be: "Take these prescribed steps and you will succeed." But such a method can very easily mould itself into a culture of works of self-righteousness. Righteousness ought to come out of relationship with God. Robert Mulholland asks a very pertinent question: "Do we seek to function out of our relationship with God, or do we try to function ourselves into a relationship with God?"[56] When Ananias and Sapphira wanted to be part of that great and exciting experience the church was demonstrating, they tried to enter into it by showing how dedicated they were in their service for God (Acts 5) but their actions were a display of fake righteousness without relationship. Such a mentality is very common today in the Western church and needs to be recognized as a hindrance to the work of growing the church.

---

56 M. Robert Mulholland Jr. *Sharpened by the Word,* Upper Room Books, Nashville, TN, 2000, p.93

In discipleship, people must be directed into a growing relationship with God, allowing good works to come out of that relationship. Deepening the relationship with God by the use of Scripture is the objective of discipleship. We can only imagine how relational the folk in the church were in Acts 2:42–47 in order to go out to other communities to spread the church.

I have tried to point to one of the key elements in Christian growth and service. As Pastor Visconti said, "You can follow Jesus for yourself, but not by yourself." This statement points to a nurturing quality, an imperative element in the process of discipleship.

In that framework, the need for the ongoing instruction and accountability must be recognized and practised. There is a false tenderness that consigns a person to sin by not holding them accountable. The one who holds another to account is showing true compassion. That is what discipleship does. It requires an intentional and compassionate commitment to the spiritual wellbeing of others, and to the spiritual growth of the church of Jesus Christ.

ABOUT THE AUTHOR

The author, Jake Giesbrecht BA MA, served as pastor, and on
the board of directors of various mission agencies .He has taught
seminars on discipleship, and a counselling course in a seminary
in Indonesia.